The Witness of Poetry

The Charles Eliot Norton Lectures

1981–82

The Witness
of Poetry

Czeslaw Milosz

Harvard University Press

Cambridge, Massachusetts

London, England • 1983

Library of Congress Cataloging in Publication Data
Miłosz, Czesław.
  The witness of poetry.

  (The Charles Eliot Norton lectures; 1981–1982)
  Includes index.
   1. Poetry—Addresses, essays, lectures.   2. Literature
and society—Addresses, essays, lectures.   I. Title.   II. Series
PN1081.M5   1983   809.1   82-15471
ISBN 0-674-95382-7

Contents

1
Starting from My Europe   *1*

2
Poets and the Human Family   *21*

3
The Lesson of Biology   *39*

4
A Quarrel with Classicism   *59*

5
Ruins and Poetry   *77*

6
On Hope   *99*

Index   *119*

Zgubiło się pokolenie. Także miasta. Narody.
Ale to trochę później. Tymczasem w oknie jaskółka.
Odprawia obrzęd sekundy. Ten chłopiec, czy już podejrzewa
Że piękność zawsze nie tu i zawsze kłamliwa?
Teraz widzi swoje powiaty. Koszą otawy.
Drogi kręte, pod górę, w dół. Borki. Jeziora.
Pochmurne niebo z jednym ukośnym promieniem.
I wszędzie rzędy kosiarzy w koszulach z grubego płótna,
W ciemnoniebieskich spodniach, barwionych wedle zwyczaju.
Widzi co widzę dotychczas. Był jednak przebiegły,
Patrzył jakby od razu rzeczy zmieniała pamięć.
Odwracał się jadąc bryką bo chciał najwięcej zachować.
To znaczy zbierał co trzeba na jakiś ostatni moment
Kiedy z okruchów ułoży świat już doskonały.

My generation was lost. Cities too. And nations.
But all this a little later. Meanwhile, in the window, a swallow
Performs its rite of the second. That boy, does he already suspect
That beauty is always elsewhere and always delusive?
Now he sees his homeland. At the time of the second mowing.
Roads winding uphill and down. Pine groves. Lakes.
An overcast sky with one slanting ray.
And everywhere men with scythes, in shirts of unbleached linen
And the dark-blue trousers that were common in the province.
He sees what I see even now. Oh but he was clever,
Attentive, as if things were instantly changed by memory.
Riding in a cart, he looked back to retain as much as possible.
Which means he knew what was needed for some ultimate moment
When he would compose from fragments a world perfect at last.

I
Starting from My Europe

MANY learned books on poetry have been written, and they find, at least in the countries of the West, more readers than does poetry itself. This is not a good sign, even if it may be explained both by the brilliance of their authors and by their zeal in assimilating scientific disciplines which today enjoy universal respect. A poet who would like to compete with those mountains of erudition would have to pretend he possesses more self-knowledge than poets are allowed to have. Frankly, all my life I have been in the power of a daimonion, and how the poems dictated by him came into being I do not quite understand. That is the reason why, in my years of teaching Slavic literatures, I have limited myself to the history of literature, trying to avoid poetics.

Yet there is something that comforts me and justifies, I think, my presence in the chair of poetry at Harvard. I have in mind the corner of Europe that shaped me and to which I have remained faithful by writing in the language of my childhood. The twentieth century, perhaps more protean and multifaceted than any other, changes according to the point from which we view it, a point in the geographic sense as well. My corner of Europe, owing to the extraordinary and lethal events that have been occurring there, comparable only to violent earthquakes, affords a peculiar perspective. As a result, all of us who come from those parts appraise poetry slightly different than do the majority of my audience, for we tend to view it as a witness and participant in one of mankind's major transformations. I have titled this book *The Witness of Poetry* not because we witness it, but because it witnesses us.

Both individuals and human societies are constantly discovering new dimensions accessible only to direct experience. This also applies to the historical dimension, which we apprehend unintentionally and even against our will. (It does not occur through books, even though historical experience does transform our reading.) By experience I mean not only feeling the direct pressure of History, with a capital H, in the form of fire falling from the sky, invasions by foreign armies, or ruined cities. Historicity may reveal itself in a detail of architecture, in the shaping of a landscape, even in trees like those oaks close to my birthplace which remember my pagan ancestors. Yet only an awareness of the dangers menacing what we love allows us to sense the dimension of time and to feel in everything we see and touch the presence of past generations.

I was born and grew up on the very borderline between Rome and Byzantium. Is it possible—one cannot help asking—to invoke today those ancient, no more than symbolic, powers? And yet that division has persisted for centuries, tracing a line, though not always on the map, between the domain of Roman Catholicism and that of Eastern Christianity. For centuries Europe maintained that old division and submitted to the law of parallel axes, a Western one which extended north from Italy and an Eastern one extending north from Byzantium. On my side of the border everything came from Rome: Latin as the language of the Church and of literature, the theological quarrels of the Middle Ages, Latin poetry as a model for the Renaissance poets, white churches in the baroque style. Also it was to the South, to Italy, that admirers of arts and letters directed their longings. Now, as I try to say something sensible about poetry, these are far from abstract considerations. If one of my themes will be the strange fate of the religious imagination, as well as the fate of poetry when it began to acquire features of a substitute religion, it is precisely because in the *gymnasium* for several years I studied the history of the Roman Church and dogmatics from thick textbooks that have since been abandoned everywhere; I doubt whether such detailed books are used now even in seminaries. Also classicism, the subject of both my fascination and my dislike, has its origin in Horace, Vergil, and Ovid, whom I read and translated in class. In my lifetime Latin disappeared from the liturgy and from high-school curricula, as a result of a gradual weakening of the South-North axis. It would be too early, however, to relegate Rome and Byzantium to the irretrievable past, since their heritage constantly takes on new forms, often difficult to define.

I certainly felt a sense of menace from the East very early, and not from Eastern Christianity, of course, but from what had arisen as a result of its defeat. The law of the South-North axis was at work not only in the case of the barbarian peoples converted by Rome, but also in the vast territories that had taken religion from Byzantium: religion, but not the language of the Church. The Russian historian Georgy Fedotov sees the source of all Russia's misfortunes in its having chosen a Slavic idiom for its Church language instead of Greek, which could have become in the East an equivalent of the West's universal Latin. Russia was thus isolated for a long time until it suddenly and belatedly discovered Western ideas, giving them grotesque and ugly shapes. In Poland, which won the war of 1920 with revolutionary Russia and succeeded in preserving its independence until 1939, the feeling of danger was too elemental to require research into its historical causes. Nevertheless, my knowledge of the Russian language since childhood, as well as some non-Western elements in my own makeup, has gradually led me to a reflection on Russian messianism and its holy city, Moscow, a city once called the third Rome (which fact has not been without consequences). Thus my interest in Dostoevsky, whose name I will pronounce here quite often, results to a large extent from geography.

The South-North axis. The language of the Polish poets of the sixteenth century, like the language of the newly translated bibles, both Catholic and Protestant, is closer to today's Polish than the language of *The Faerie Queene* is to today's English. Or, if you prefer, it is closer in tone and sensibility. This means that a Polish poet has a more intimate relationship with his predecessors in the poetic craft and feels at home in the sixteenth century. But the most eminent among those poets, Jan Kochanowski, was bilingual; he wrote a number of poems in Latin, and many of his Polish poems are just adaptations from Horace. A Polish poet is thus constantly reminded of that very professional question: what should be done today with classicism?

The notion of the South-North axis is, I hope, clear enough. Another notion, the West-East axis, is perhaps more exotic, though not for readers of *War and Peace*, for instance, where the heroes, well-educated Russians, happily converse in French. In the eighteenth century French becomes, after Latin, the second universal language of Europe, and this time Russia was included in its range. In provincial East and Central European capitals a myth was born, of Paris, the capital of the world. The eyes of devout Catholics might still have been turned to Rome, the capital of the papacy. But the enlightened, the worldly, the chasers of fashion, all wanted to know what had just happened in Parisian intellectual salons. France exported in succession its philosophers, its revolution, war under Napoleon, then its novel, and finally a revolution in poetry and painting: symbolism, cubism, fauvism, surrealism. Now all this seems to be a period closed or approaching its close, for, just as Latin disappeared from the churches and schools, fewer and fewer of Europe's young people consider it worthwhile, even for the sake of snobbery, to learn French. Yet the modern poetry of many European countries can be understood only if we keep in mind a fusion of two metals—one of native origin, the other imported from Paris.

The literary map of Europe, as it presented itself to the West, contained until recently numerous blank spots. England, France, Germany, and Italy had a definite place, but the Iberian peninsula was no more than a vague outline; Holland, Belgium, and Scandinavia were blurred; while to the east of Germany the white space could have easily borne the inscription *Ubi leones* (Where the lions are), and that domain of wild beasts included such cities as Prague (mentioned sometimes because of Kafka), Warsaw, Budapest, and Belgrade. Only farther to the east does Moscow appear on the map. The images preserved by a cultural elite undoubtedly also have political significance as they influence the decisions of the groups that govern, and it is no wonder that the statesmen who signed the Yalta agreement so easily wrote off a hundred million Europeans from these blank areas in the loss column. Perhaps it was then that a definite break occurred on the West-East axis, and Parisian intellectuals, used to having their ideas and books admired for their universality beyond the Vistula, the Dnieper, and the Danube, woke up to find themselves sentenced to provincialism. They started to search for some compensation on the other side of the Atlantic, where, however, their involuted style and thought did not find many followers, even at the universities.

In my youth, apprentices in poetry, if they came from the blank spots on the map, had to undergo a short or a longer period of training in Paris. That was the case with me, strengthened by some family precedent, for a relative of mine, a distant cousin, Oscar Milosz, brought up in France, was a French poet. Arriving in Paris as a young man, I later had many opportunities to wonder at the contrast between the radical changes occurring in myself and in my geographical zone to the east of Germany, on the one hand, and the perfect stability and the continuity in the life of *la ville lumière* on the other. Half a century later I wrote a poem on that subject, which better explains what I just said than does my prose.

BYPASSING RUE DESCARTES

Bypassing rue Descartes
I descended toward the Seine, shy, a traveler,
A young barbarian just come to the capital of the world.

We were many, from Jassy and Koloshvar, Wilno and Bucharest, Saigon and Marakesh,
Ashamed to remember the customs of our homes,
About which nobody here should ever be told:
The clapping for servants, barefoot girls hurry in,
Dividing food with incantations,
Choral prayers recited by masters and household together.

I had left the cloudy provinces behind,
I entered the universal, dazzled and desiring.

Soon enough, many from Jassy and Koloshvar, or Saigon or Marakesh
Were killed because they wanted to abolish the customs of their homes.

Soon enough, their peers were seizing power
In order to kill in the name of the universal beautiful ideas.

Meanwhile, the city behaved in accordance with its nature,
Rustling with throaty laughter in the dark,
Baking long breads and pouring wine into clay pitchers,
Buying fish, lemons and garlic at street markets,
Indifferent as it was to honor and shame and greatness and glory,
Because that had been done and transformed itself
Into monuments representing nobody knows whom,
Into arias hardly audible and into turns of speech.

Again I lean on the rough granite of the embankment,
As if I had returned from travels through the underworlds
And suddenly saw in the light the reeling wheel of the seasons
Where empires have fallen and those once living are now dead.

There is no capital of the world, neither here nor anywhere else,
And the abolished customs are restored to their small fame,
And I know the time of human generations is not like the time
   of the earth.

As to my heavy sins, I remember one most vividly:
How, one day, walking a forest path along a stream,
I pushed a rock down onto a water snake coiled in the grass.

And what I have met with in life was the just punishment
Which reaches, sooner or later, everyone who breaks a taboo.

Though universal ideas long ago lost their appeal for those
of us from Wilno, Warsaw, or Budapest, this does not mean
they lost their appeal everywhere. The young cannibals who,
in the name of inflexible principles, butchered the population
of Cambodia had graduated from the Sorbonne and were simply trying to implement the philosophic ideas they had
learned. As for ourselves, since we had seen firsthand what
one achieves by violating, in the name of doctrine, local mores
(that is everything which grows slowly, organically, for centuries), we could only think with horror about the absurdities
haunting the human mind, indifferent as it is to the repetitive
character of blunders.

The poem I read has a few themes. Its main layer is a confession, an avowal of grave sin. Not because to kill any living
creature is evil—but because I come from Lithuania where the
water snake was considered holy. Bowls of milk were set out
for them at the thresholds of peasants' huts. People associated
them with fertility, fertility of the soil and of the family, and
the Sun loved the water snake. There is a Lithuanian folk say-
ing: "Do not leave a dead *żaltys* on a field; bury it. The sight of
a dead *żaltys* would cause the sun to cry."*

Certainly, the student who wrote his French copositions
zealously and read Paul Valéry should not have had much in

* Quoted by Marija Gimbutas in "Ancient Symbolism in Lithuanian Folk
Art," *Memoirs of the American Folklore Society,* 49 (Philadelphia, 1958).

common with the cult of snakes. And yet the superstitious side of my nature was and is stronger than the universal ideas, at least on the level where poetry is born. Though Roman Catholicism inculcated me with a permanent sense of sin, perhaps another, more primitive, pagan notion proved to be stronger, that of guilt from violation of the sacred.

I do not intend to go too far in stressing such provincial exoticism. One of the strangest regularities to be taken into account by a historian of literature and art is the affinity binding people who live at the same time in countries distant from one another. I am even inclined to believe that the mysterious substance of time itself determines the similarities of a given historical moment even between civilizations not in communication. Such a thesis may appear farfetched; let me therefore limit myself to Europe. There the mark of a common style binds contemporaneous poets writing in various languages, which may be explained by an elusive osmosis and not necessarily by direct borrowings. But borrowings have been common. For instance, at the turn of the sixteenth and seventeenth centuries a Frenchman was able to read a poem on the ruins of Rome signed Joachim du Bellay; a Pole knew the same poem as the work of Mikołaj Sęp-Szarzyński; a Spaniard, as the work of Francesco de Quevedo; while the true author, whom the others adapted without scruple, was a little-known Latin humanist, Ianus Vitalis of Palermo. The acceleration of exchanges made the osmosis and mutual borrowings among the poets of the twentieth century obvious, so that Warsaw or Budapest, or my Wilno, was not outside a certain circuit. Even in distant New York, the literary groups of the nineteen-thirties, with their leftism, Marxism, and "literature for the masses," faithfully repeated the main concerns of the literati in my province. Besides, literary New York was composed mostly of immigrants from Eastern and Central Europe.

In addition to the South-North and West-East axes, there is a third I would like to discuss: the Past-Future axis. In our time we have quite often heard that poetry is a palimpsest that, when properly decoded, provides testimony to its epoch. Such an assertion is correct, however—on condition that it not be applied in the manner preferred by Marxist-oriented schools of sociology, including the sociology of literature. Having spent time in the limbo of social doctrines, I know their sterility too well to return to them here, even though I did once observe them being applied most ingeniously—and comically—in the quarrels of the Polish avant-garde of the twenties over which kind of rhyme is socialist. I do not doubt, though, that posterity will read us in an attempt to comprehend what the twentieth century was like, just as we learn much about the nineteenth century from the poems of Rimbaud and the prose of Flaubert.

Clearly I am reflecting upon what sort of testimony about our century is being established by poetry, though I realize we are still submerged in our time and our judgments should be assessed in advance as uncertain. Let me approach this topic in a roundabout manner beginning with Mozart's opera *The Magic Flute* and a film by Ingmar Bergman with the same title, a film that better perhaps than any other demonstrates what film art is capable of, especially now when its technical perfection is primarily used to debase man. *The Magic Flute* introduces us to a climate so radically different from that in which we live that the very contrast between the aura of the late eighteenth century and that of our time is instructive. The libretto of the Mozart opera deals with a struggle between the darkness of obscurantism and the light of reason; the sacred and the rational are not separated, for the Temple, in other words, the Freemasonic lodge, bestows sacral features on the human mind in search of Wisdom. That Wisdom, besides, was conceived in various ways, as exemplified by the proliferation throughout the eighteenth century of "mystical lodges," convincingly presented in a classical work on the subject, *Les Sources occultes du romantisme* by Auguste Viatte. In *The Magic*

Flute man wins access to the Temple after he passes through trials and initiations. Those who do not succumb to the treacherous charms of the Queen of the Night will find themselves among the chosen few united by a common purpose, sharing knowledge about how to secure happiness for the people. The opera, let us note, had its premiere in Vienna in 1791, the year when a constitution was voted in Warsaw, and that too was the work of Freemasons and one of the offshoots of the French Revolution.

The people of that period seem to breathe confidence and hope, as well as faith in the approach of a new era for humanity; for some it seemed a millennium. Many of them would lose their heads on the guillotine. Others would follow Napoleon, experiencing his defeat as the end of all hope for a long time. Still others would write programs of utopian socialism. All of them, though, were animated by the renewed and secularized idea expressed quite early by a medieval monk, Joachim di Fiore, who divided history into three epochs: the epoch of the Father, the epoch of the Son, and the epoch to come, of the Spirit.

Even today it is still not clear what, in fact, the phenomenon called romanticism was, especially since the term does not mean the same in England and on the Continent and, moreover, means different things in different European countries. Romantic poetry is the very core of Polish literature. I grew up and completed my studies in the city of Wilno where Polish romanticism was born, probably not by chance, considering the peculiar character of the Lithuanian capital. In my youth it continued to be a city of churches and of Freemasonic lodges, and it seemed that the carriage of Napoleon, who had passed through in his march on Moscow, had departed only yesterday. My elder university colleagues—elder by a hundred years—founded secret organizations of the initiated, like that in *The Magic Flute*. One of them became the greatest of Polish poets, and I consider myself, of course, his disciple. I have come from a blank spot on the map, and so in citing the name of Adam Mickiewicz I cannot expect my audience to have any associations: that name is virtually unknown in the West. Had I mentioned the poet Alexander Pushkin it would have been otherwise. But the greatness of Pushkin is taken on faith, for translations give no idea of his high quality; his reputation was reinforced by that of the great Russian prose writers. His Polish contemporary, Mickiewicz, is equally untranslatable. His verse resumes in a way the whole history of Polish verse, which first was shaped by Latin classicism, then by French classicism of the Enlightenment. It is not only poetic technique that makes Mickiewicz an inheritor of the Enlightenment. In him, the philosophy of *les lumières* is both negated and accepted as a basic optimism toward the future, a millenarian faith in the epoch of the Spirit. In many countries this seems to provide a link between the Age of Reason and the first half of the nineteenth century, which I would call the Age of Raptures. William Blake, a poet hostile to the rationalism of philosophers, cannot be understood if we bypass his prophecies on the victory of man in his struggle against the night, the cold, and the spectral ego.

On the borderline of Rome and Byzantium, Polish poetry became a home for incorrigible hope, immune to historical disasters. Only in appearance does that hope date either from the time when Mozart wrote *The Magic Flute* or from the Age of Raptures. In reality its roots reach a few centuries further back. It seems to draw its strength from a belief in the basic goodness of the world sustained by the hand of God and by the poetry of country people. The major work of Polish literature is a tale in verse, *Pan Tadeusz* by Mickiewicz, written in the years 1832–1834 in Paris by a political emigré. The poem, whose setting is the Lithuanian countryside, celebrates the delights of gathering mushrooms and preparing tasty coffee, describes hunts and feasts, speaks with admiration of trees as if they were persons, and ascribes peculiar meaning to sunrises and sunsets, which are seen as a curtain rising and falling in a serene and comic theater of dolls. Unique in its genre, an amazing achievement in world poetry, the poem has retained its position as the bedside book of every Polish poet, and may even be responsible for the contents of this lecture.

This leads me back to the Past-Future axis. The fate of poetry depends on whether such a work as Schiller's and Beethoven's "Ode to Joy" is possible. For that to be so, some basic confidence is needed, a sense of open space ahead of the individual and the human species. How did it happen that to be a poet of the twentieth century means to receive training in every kind of pessimism, sarcasm, bitterness, doubt? In this respect there is no great difference between the years of my youth and the present time, when the century is drawing to its close. Perhaps the specific trait of these last decades is that negative attitudes have become so widespread that the poets have been overtaken by the man in the street. As a youth I felt the complete absurdity of everything occurring on our planet, a nightmare that could not end well—and in fact it found its perfect expression in the barbed wire around the concentration camps and gas chambers. Brought up on Polish romantics, I obviously had to search for the causes of that contrast between their open future and our future laden with catastrophe. Today I think that, while the list of dreaded apocalyptic events may change, what is constant is a certain state of mind. This state precedes the perception of specific reasons for despair, which come later.

Let us take a few American examples. In a country whose founding fathers professed the philosophy of the Enlightenment, Walt Whitman was no anomaly. He was a poet for whom the future was as open as it had been both in the Age of Reason and in the Age of Raptures. But a couple of decades after his death, everything changes. The expatriate poets hate the present and the future; they turn their eyes to the past. It is difficult to find any tomorrow in T. S. Eliot's *The Waste Land,*

and where there is no tomorrow, moralizing makes its entrance. The very chaos of ideas in his friend Ezra Pound's *Cantos* proclaims a reactionary political option. Robinson Jeffers, self-exiled to the shores of the Pacific, hostile to society, creates visions of a heroic "inhumanism," in which there is no place for the dimension of the future:

> Observe also
> How rapidly civilization coarsens and decays; its better
>   qualities, foresight, humaneness, disinterested
> Respect for truth die first; the worst will be last
>   ("Teheran" in *The Double Axe*)

Though quite differently—I would say inversely—motivated, Allen Ginsberg's *Howl* crowns the history of Whitmanesque verse which once served to sing of the open road ahead. Instead we now have despair at the imprisonment of man in an evil civilization, in a trap without release.

It is not easy to separate this loss of hope from the causes either advanced by writers or guessed at by critics. I assume that we are dealing here with something real, not with an illusion, and for the moment I will abstain from interpretation, heaping together examples that at first glance will have little in common except a dark coloring.

I hear an objection, and it is my own too. After all, this is a century of utopian hope. In its name people have been dying, in its name people have been killing each other—and that hope has taken the form of a revolution whose goal is to replace the ominous power of money with a state monopoly and a planned economy. The vertical orientation, when man turned his eyes toward Heaven, has gradually been replaced in Europe during the last few centuries by a horizontal longing: the always spatial human imagination has replaced "above" with "ahead,"and that "ahead" is claimed by Marxism. The Russian revolution unleashed great energies and great expectations everywhere. There were, however, many disappointments in store. Artists, writers, and scholars proved most sensitive to the promise of a new world and of a new man, and so their hopes were exposed to particularly hard trials. The civil war in Spain demonstrated their dilemma: "If you are against fascism, you are with us; therefore you must approve of the Soviet totalitarian system." The dilemma is still being repeated. Living for many years in Paris I observed the desperate efforts of my French colleagues to maintain their faith in the quick fulfillment of History's goals, in spite of the obvious facts.

Does this mean that hope pervades our century? Perhaps, but poetry does not confirm that impression, and it is a more reliable witness than journalism. If something cannot be verified on a deeper level, that of poetry, it is not, we may suspect, authentic. The opinions of authors are not, as we know, a reliable key to their work. Their works may even contradict their opinions. In our century many writers opted for revolution, but in their writings man has not been presented as deserving transformation but is depicted instead as a bedbug, the title of one of Mayakovsky's plays. They justify that dark picture by invoking their major task, that of criticizing capitalism. And yet, in the case of Bertolt Brecht for example, acidity and scorn so penetrate the very core of his plays, that the clear consciousness accessible to man as postulated by Brecht reminds us of the hypothetical salvation in those Christian authors who in reality delight in descriptions of sin.

One can advance the thesis that the inhumanity of life in the conditions of a market economy is responsible for the somber image of man in literature and art. After all, Brecht is primarily a poet of the Weimar Republic, which begot Nazism, just as in painting George Grosz is its portraitist. Yes, but surely it is high time now, sixty-six years after the Russian revolution, to find some optimism in the poetry of the countries called socialist. Just as the opinions of poets often are in disagreement with what issues from their pens, so rhetoric often passes for poetry and is its temporary substitute. After the revolution Mayakovsky writes rhetoric amazing in its giantism. The truth, however, does not reside there but in the soft-spoken poems of Osip Mandelstam and in those of Anna Akhmatova who, in postrevolutionary Russia, saw Dostoevsky's most depressing forebodings confirmed. Akhmatova wrote, "The prisoner of Omsk understood everything and gave up on everything." Nor does the poetry of the countries that were placed in the Soviet orbit after the Second World War bear out any of the joyous promises made by the system. On the contrary, irony and sarcasm are distilled by poetry, for instance in Poland, to a very high degree, though that poetry is one of rebellion, which fact, paradoxically, keeps it alive.

So we do not seem to commit an error if we hear a minor mode in the poetry of our century. I suspect that a poet writing in another mode would be considered old-fashioned and accused of living in a fool's paradise. Yet it is one thing to live in a limbo of doubt and dejection, another to like it. Certain states of mind are not normal, in the sense that they turn against some real, not imaginery, laws of human nature. We cannot feel well if we know that we are forbidden to move forward along a straight line, if everywhere we knock against a wall that forces us to swerve and to return to the point of departure, in other words, to walk in a circle. Yet to realize that the poetry of the twentieth century testifies to serious disturbances in our perception of the world may already become the first step in self-therapy.

What matters is to gain some distance on certain attitudes too universally taken for granted, to learn to mistrust some habits we can no longer even see. If it is fashionable today to investigate the linguistic structures characteristic of one or another historical period, trying to find to what extent they determine that period's whole way of thinking, there is no reason why we should not direct our suspicions against our own century as well. The grounds for gloom, as voiced by poets, should in a way be taken parenthetically, at least until we are able to discuss them together with those factors that are less often mentioned. Since I have hinted at self-therapy, I should add that by reflecting on pessimism we have no guarantee of a positive result, for we may come to recognize it as, partly at least, justified.

We may advance the hypothesis that the gloom in the poetry of our century has been gradually increasing and that when looking for its causes we must go back to the poetry of our predecessors. Today a poet is aware that modern poetry has its own history, its ancestors, heroes, and martyrs. It was no coincidence that Baudelaire, Rimbaud, and Mallarmé were Frenchmen, for the birth of their poetry came at a time when French was still the language of European culture. The new poetry was born out of a deep schism within that culture, out of a clash between diametrically opposed philosophies and ways of life. With the year 1848 the Age of Raptures came to its close and the Age of Progress began. That was the season of the victorious scientific Weltanschauung, positivism, new inventions joyously accepted, the triumphant march of technology. But the underground already existed, and the underground knew that a worm was hidden in the beautiful apple. The voice of the underground is heard in Dostoevsky and in Nietzsche, who predicted the ascent of what he called European nihilism. In poetry, bohemia proclaimed its disagreement, trying to oppose average mortals, the bourgeoisie, with its own different scale of values, even different dress, and dividing people into the elect, worthy of receiving the sacrament of art, on the one hand, and ordinary bread eaters on the other. What is essential here is the conviction, lucidly formulated by the French symbolists, that the scale of values still professed by "right-thinking" citizens was already dead, that its foundation, religion, had been hollowed out from inside, and that art was going to take over its function and become the only dwelling place of the sacred. The symbolists discovered the idea of a poem as an autonomous, self-sufficient unit, no longer describing the world but existing *instead* of the world.

The poetry of the twentieth century inherited the basic quarrel between bohemian and philistine, something we should not forget. It was not the best preparation for the encounter with a reality that grew more gigantic and more ominous with every decade, increasingly eluding the grasp of the mind. The heritage of bohemia provides an explanation of at least some features of modern and postmodern poetry that make it very different from the poetry written in the name of hope.

2
Poets and the Human Family

IN THE first half of the twentieth century there was a
French poet completely out of step with the notions on
poetry that were then current. In his lifetime he was known
only to a small group of poet-friends. During the decades
since his death in the spring of 1939, his renown has spread to
larger circles, and his works have been translated into several
languages. He has remained, though, a writer for a relatively
limited public. That poet, Oscar Milosz or, as he used to sign
his name, O. V. de L. Milosz, came from the Grand Duchy of
Lithuania and was a distant relative of mine. I invoke him here
because I want to present his views on poetry, which I feel are
of considerable relevance.

Since he is virtually unknown in English-speaking countries, I must introduce him briefly. In America, which was for
him the land of his lifelong friend Christian Gauss of Princeton, only one slim volume of his poems has appeared, in 1955,
translated by Kenneth Rexroth, and today it is a bibliophilic
rarity. A French poet in spite of his exotic origin, like Guillaume Appollinaire-Kostrowicki, Oscar Milosz, born in 1877,
was at the time of his debut in 1899 considered part of the second wave of symbolists. And thus a certain choice he made

seems all the more strange: of his own accord, he dwelled spiritually in an earlier era in European history, the late eighteenth and early nineteenth centuries, and he mistrusted what happened later to European civilization. His cosmopolitan education might have been a contributing factor since he knew several languages well, and in his youth he was under the spell of German poetry, of Heine and above all of Goethe, then of Hölderlin, whom he discovered in 1914.

Be that as it may, his assessment of his own era was negative. He called his century "an age of jeering ugliness," and the images of the present in his poems are no more cheerful than are Eliot's or Pound's. There is, however, something that causes him to differ radically from those representatives of modern poetry: his millenarianism, his belief in the advent of a new epoch—whatever name we may give it—Blake's New Jerusalem or the Epoch of Spirit of the continental romantics. According to Oscar Milosz's philosophical writings, this new age would occur after an apocalyptic catastrophe, which he placed around 1944. What he called "la conflagration universelle" perhaps signified the explosion of atomic weapons, an event unimaginable in the 1920s and 1930s. As to the new epoch, we still are waiting for it. According to him, such a renaissance would be accomplished by a new science, one that would shed Newtonian physics and draw radical philosophical conclusions from Einstein's discoveries. But I am not concerned here with the truth or error of these predictions. It is enough to say that, because of his orientation toward the future, he belonged to a family that includes both William Blake and the Polish romantics. He believed that he would be read and understood by distant generations, happier than his own, for they would live in a time when harmony between man and the universe had been recovered. He kept his distance from contemporary poetry, in which he saw an image of total confusion. I have never concealed that my acquaintance with his writings when I was a young man, as well as our personal contact, to a large extent determined my own ways as a poet, inclining me to resist literary fashions. Here I would like to analyze one of Oscar Milosz's works, *A Few Words on Poetry*, dated somewhere between 1930 and 1937 and published in France many years later, after the death of its author. It presents in concise form the views that may be found in his other books as well.

In the preamble poetry is defined as a companion of man since his beginnings, since the magic rituals of cave dwellers. It has always been "an organizer of the archetypes" and—for my purposes, most important—"a passionate pursuit of the Real":

> That sacred art of the Word, just because it springs forth from the sacred depths of Universal Being, appears to us as bound, more rigorously than any other mode of expression, to the spiritual and physical Movement of which it is a generator and a guide. And precisely for that reason it separated itself from Music, a language that, since the dawn of Panhellenism, has been primarily affective, and, thus separated, it has taken part in the incessant transformations of religious, political and social thought, and dominated them. Sacerdotal in prehistoric times, epic at the moment of Greek colonial expansion, psychological and tragic at the decline of the dionysia, Christian, theological and sentimental in the Middle Ages, neoclassical since the beginning of the first spiritual and political revolution—namely the Renaissance—finally romantic, i.e., both mystical and social before and after 1789, poetry has always followed, fully aware of its terrible responsibilities, the mysterious movements of the great soul of the people (*la grande âme populaire*).

Poetry is an art of rhythm but is not primarily an affective means of communication like music. Its language enables it to participate in and to dominate "the incessant transformations of religious, political and social thought." Oscar Milosz's model of time is dynamic, as is William Blake's, and historical movement takes the form of a triad: the time of innocence, the time of the fall, and the time of innocence recovered. And in yet another aspect this French poet remained faithful to the epoch of romanticism, which he chose as his own: poetry must be aware of its "terrible responsibilities," for it is not a purely individual game and it gives shape to the aspirations of "the great soul of the people." It is here probably that we should seek the causes of Oscar Milosz's alienation from his contemporary French milieu. Highly fastidious, aristocratic, a late symbolist by his very life style, he did not seek social programs that might secure him allies. At the same time, he did not believe poetry could turn its back on the public with impunity:

> After Goethe and Lamartine—the great, very great, Lamartine of "The Death of Socrates"—poetry, under the influence of charming romantic minor German poets, as well as that of Edgar Poe, Baudelaire and Mallarmé, suffered a kind of impoverishment and narrowing, which oriented it, in the domain of the subconscious, toward an undoubtedly interesting, sometimes even remarkable, search which has been, however, tainted with preoccupations of an aesthetic and nearly always individualistic order. Besides, that little solitary exercise has not resulted, in nine hundred and ninety poets in a thousand, in any more than purely verbal finds constituted by unforeseen associations of words and not expressing any internal, mental or spiritual operation. This unfortunate deviation produced a schism and a misunderstanding between the poet and the great human family, which has continued to the present and will not end until a great, inspired poet appears, a modern Homer, Shakespeare or Dante, initiated, through the renunciation of his paltry ego, his often empty and always cramped ego, into the most profound secret of the laboring masses, more than ever alive, vibrant and tormented.

Twentieth-century poetry suffered "impoverishment and narrowing" because its interests became limited to "an aesthetic and nearly always individualistic order." In other words, it withdrew from the domain common to all people into the closed circle of subjectivism. I am aware of the terminological trap here, for the author is obviously opposing the individual's perceptions to a world that exists objectively. Yet we understand, more or less, what he has in mind. He disapproves of poetry that is no more than a "little solitary exercise," and he requires a poem to be an expression of what he calls an internal operation. By this he probably means the act of universalizing personal experiences. Milosz thus attacks one of the basic tenets of modern poetics which was codified by the French symbolists and has been reappearing since then in several forms. This is the belief that true art cannot be understood by ordinary people. But who are those ordinary people? A whole social structure is reflected in such a belief. In the France of the nineteenth century neither workers nor peasants were counted among the consumers of art. What remained was the bourgeoisie with its bad taste, which perhaps reached its height in the tombstones in the Père Lachaise cemetery. For the bohemians that class became an object of hatred, and they regarded writing as an activity directed against it. If Oscar Milosz mentioned Mallarmé as a promoter of aestheticism, he could have mentioned Flaubert as well, for whom the will to contradict the bourgeoisie is at the very core of his creative work. But was Flaubert contradicting the bourgeoisie or contradicting life? This is not clear because for Flaubert ordinary people epitomized life in general, which was as dreary as the existence of woodlice. The separation of art and the public has been an accomplished fact ever since. In various schools and manifestoes of the twentieth century there was a division into two camps: on one side those who earn and spend, with their cult of work, their religion and patriotism, and, on the other, the bohemians whose religion is art and whose morality is the negation of all values recognized by the other camp. Certain movements, like the flower children in the United States, represent a miraculous multiplication of bohemian attitudes. In Europe, since the middle of the nineteenth century, the poet has been an alien, an asocial individual, at best a member of a subculture. And this has perpetuated "the schism and the misunderstanding between the poet and the great human family." The author of *A Few Words on Poetry* was far from being a Marxist, and his words should not be construed as a call for socially committed poetry. Nevertheless, he was of the opinion that the future belongs to the workers, and he considered the culture of the upper classes decadent. The truly *inspired* poet of the future will transcend his paltry ego (his "spectral self," as William Blake would say) and, in contrast to the poets of the elite, would voice the unconscious longings of downtrodden people who were now being emancipated. He would penetrate "the most profound secret of the laboring masses, more than ever alive, vibrant and tormented." To quote more from Oscar Milosz:

> And thus, for about one century, the activity of the literati expressing themselves in verse or in a rhythmical prose has been, practically in its entirety, set under the sign of a search for "pure poetry." These two words betray a somewhat childish preoccupation on the part of those who bring them together, and more precision is needed. Unfortunately, the words become more or less intelligible only after a long process of elimination. If they have any meaning at all, they denote a poetry that would remove religion, philosophy, science, politics from its domain, and even eliminate the influences which may have been exerted upon the poet by the methods and tendencies of all the other branches of art. Thus "pure poetry" would be a poetry of spontaneity, and would be of the most profound and the most direct sort.

In this passage the attack is directed against the sacrosanct beliefs of the elite, who reserve for themselves the ability to appreciate "pure art," while the philistines are left with an art that is thematic, sentimental, and melodramatic. More or less at the same time, Ortega y Gasset wrote his famous essay "The Dehumanization of Art," and pure poetry was canonized when, in 1925, under the cupola of the French Academy, l'abbé Henri Brémond delivered his lecture on that subject. He declared that pure poetry consists of an ineffable combination of sounds as in magic incantations, regardless of their meaning, and as an example of pure poetry he quoted a line from Racine: "La fille de Minos et de Pasiphaé." Pure poetry parallels similar attempts to liberate painting from "content" and from the imitation of nature. Various branches of art competed in that striving toward purity, sometimes with surprising effects. If music takes such a course rather easily and painting tends to abstraction, it is more difficult to imagine "pure action" in the theater. Yet it was introduced in theory and, to some degree, in practice by two eccentrics working at the same time but unaware of each other—a Pole, Stanisław Ignacy Witkiewicz, and a Frenchman, Antonin Artaud.

My French cousin is not a partisan of a poetry that "would remove religion, philosophy, science, politics from its domain." And undoubtedly this is how pure poetry proceeds because, even if it uses notions and images taken from the nonpoetic activities of the human mind, it does so for its own purposes. The poets of the past were not "pure." That is, they did not assign poetry a narrow territory, did not leave religion, philosophy, science, and politics to ordinary people who supposedly were unable to share in the initiations of the elite. Again, let me return to the text: pure poetry, according to Oscar Milosz, escapes definition and denotes a kind of pure lyricism. So perhaps any attempt to define it should be abandoned:

> We may hear that pure poetry, though it appears to be elusive, does, in fact, exist and it is enough to possess the requisite faculty to discover it. We shall then humbly ask where those aristocratic spirits seek it and in which works they find it; with their elitist souls they certainly do not get intoxicated by Homer as do the porters of Naucratis or Miletus, with Dante as do the workers of Florence and the gondoliers of Venice, or by Shakespeare with his audience of London street Arabs. Pure poetry: is it Ulysses' battle with the suitors, the descent of Aeneus into Hell, Heaven in *The Divine Comedy*, *Ballade et Oraison*, *A Mid-*

summer Night's Dream, the fifth act of *Berenice,* the end of *Faust?* Is it "Ulalume," "Elegy to Diotima," "Afternoon of a Faun"? Or, more simply, is it the poetry of our time, the poetry that finds no audience, the poetry of the "unrecognized," the poetry of the mediocre such as we all without exception are, we who do not even read each other?

The author's thought is somewhat more fastidious than it appears at first glance. He speaks sarcastically of aristocratic spirits and "elitist souls," but not because those he attacks refuse to write a poetry that would *now* be accessible to Greek porters, Italian workers, or London street Arabs. Probably nobody would be able to write such poetry, for poets in the twentieth century are by nature isolated, deprived of a public, "unrecognized," while the great soul of the people is asleep, unaware of itself and learns of itself only in the poetry of the past. (Anyone who has heard simple people in Italy recite Dante's stanzas from memory realizes the great vitality of that old poetry.) As to the poets of today, they are "mediocre," all of them, including the author who also pronounces a severe verdict upon himself. But he, at least, does not fall victim to illusions, as do the elitist souls.

This raises the issue of the poets' anxiety, the anxiety that has seized them every time they have encountered the man in the street: at such moments they have sensed their own refinement, their "culture," which has made them incomprehensible; thus they have felt potentially subject to the mockery of the common man, who found their occupation unmanly. When they have tried to ingratiate themselves with him by "lowering themselves to his level," the results were not good, for poetry does not accord with such forced operations. The passage just quoted from Milosz is not normative; it merely advances a diagnosis of the phenomenon. That phenomenon is still current in the United States, for both the authors and readers of poetry come from university campuses. The proliferation of poets and students' interest in poetry should not veil the fact that behind all of this there is a mutual hostility between the elite and ordinary citizens, one that perhaps has not diminished since the time of the French *poètes maudits*. Besides, in America for instance, the sales of poetry are quite low, which is a valid indicator.

A Few Words on Poetry was written nearly half a century ago. Historical events have since proved the correctness of Oscar Milosz's diagnosis. For when an entire community is struck by misfortune, for instance, the Nazi occupation of Poland, the "schism between the poet and the great human family" disappears and poetry becomes as essential as bread. I foresee the objection that exceptional situations such as war and the Resistance can scarcely be used as a standard. Yet under the Nazi occupation, class barriers in the Polish underground began to be broken down; that was the beginning of a process intensified later on under Communist rule, until finally another society took shape, the one the world saw in the workers' strike of August 1980. In that new society it was not unusual for 150,000 copies of a book of poems to be sold out in a few hours; the division between the worker and the intellectual was waning too. In the United States a new relationship between poet and audience was adumbrated by the youth revolt of the 1960s, which has had lasting effects and, to some extent, reduced the poet's isolation.

To return to Oscar Milosz:

> It is possible to affirm, without any bias or any intention to indulge in paradoxes, that for nearly a hundred years the world has not produced one single poet, I mean, a true poet deserving to be compared to one of those big rivers equally hospitable to barges and gilded galleys, magnificently carrying in their impetuous and deep waters the better and the worse, fertile silt and sand, but always moving in a sovereign rhythm and flow that on the whole provides an image of the fixity of things divine and of the passing of generations.

A reader of these words directed against purity in poetry, and praising "impure" poetry, cannot but think of Walt Whitman, who seems to fulfill the conditions enumerated. And he must

also think Oscar Milosz is much closer to our sensibility than
he is to that of the thirties.

The next quotation calls for a commentary in advance.
Oscar Milosz was very young when, in Paris, he met Oscar
Wilde, then an old man. He calls him, in accordance with
Wilde's family origin, "an Irish poet." I should also mention
that, whereas Byron had no more admirers then than he has
today, Oscar Milosz knew many stanzas of Byron by heart.

> In essence, that search for pure poetry derives directly from the
> mannerism of the schools called "aesthetic." Under different
> names it was already the subject of our discussions, around
> 1895, in Kallisaya, the first American bar in Paris, which num-
> bered among its regular patrons my friends Oscar Wilde and
> Moréas. And I will never forget the look of disapproval, given
> me by the Irish poet, which I earned one day in the middle of a
> conversation on Shelley, that great ancestor of aestheticism, by
> voicing my preference for Byron the rhymester and disciple of
> Pope, a classical poet; Byron, who did not hesitate in his sub-
> lime *Manfred*, the most human and least romantic of poems, to
> take on the eternal Promethean theme and treat it in his own
> manner.

The poetry of his time was, according to the author of *A Few
Words on Poetry*, "a descendant of the world bourgeoisie in its
decline" and for that reason, if poetry was to exist in the future, it had to make a complete break with its direct predecessors. But this development would not depend on poetry alone.
Milosz foresaw a great transformation in all fields of human
activity, a new Renaissance; as I said, he was a millenarian.
The new Renaissance was primarily to be the result of post-
Einsteinian physics.

> The poetry of tomorrow will be born out of the scientific and
> social transmutation which is occurring before our very eyes.
> The Great War, the last or the next-to-last leap of capitalism
> and imperialism, still awaits its bard. So let poetry peacefully

arm itself with patience. It is the spiritual consequences of events and not events themselves that summon the inspired. The Russian revolution wishes to create its minstrel artificially. Yet it is not through the mechanical application of a materialist doctrine that one calls a new social order to life, and even less so makes a poet appear.

Let us recall that Emanuel Swedenborg, from whom William Blake borrowed so much, assigned the date of the Last Judgment to the year 1757, though there were no external indications that any such judgment was taking form. Similarly Blake, born in the year of the Swedenborgian Last Judgment, proclaimed in his prophetic books a millennium that would arise in secret, under the surface of phenomena, and ascribed a crucial role to himself in its preparation. Oscar Milosz did not know Blake, and the affinities between them may be explained by their common indebtedness to Swedenborg, who maintained that a scientific and social transformation was already occurring in his lifetime in preparation of a new Renaissance. From our perspective, however, I should add that World War I did not find its bard because the twenty years separating it from World War II were far too short an interval. Besides, poetry was not and is still not prepared to grasp the enormity of the crimes committed in this century, and the "spiritual consequences of events" are clear to no one. On the other hand, what Oscar Milosz says of the Russian revolution has been corroborated. The suicide of its bard, Mayakovsky, had more than personal significance. Both Mayakovsky's oeuvre and his death are marked by contradictions characteristic of the Russian intelligentsia of the preceding century, which were brought to cruel light by the revolution.

The author of *A Few Words on Poetry* predicted a prompt unification of "the small planet Earth," a new science and a new metaphysics. He even tried to imagine what the poetry of the future would be like: "The form of the new poetry will be, in all probability, that of the Bible: a spacious prose hammered into verses." Thus the state of poetry in a given epoch *may* testify to the vitality or to the drying up of the life-giving sources of civilization. By observing contemporary poetry, Oscar Milosz drew pessimistic conclusions, and it would be interesting to compare his assessments with those of T. S. Eliot or Ezra Pound or T. E. Hulme—those poets who, more or less at the same time, pronounced unfavorable verdicts on modern technological civilization. It seems that the main difference consisted in *the myth of return* present in poets with a conservative orientation. By pronouncing the names of Homer, Dante, and Shakespeare, my cousin also seemed to evidence the nostalgia that has been pervasive in different phases of our civilization: what is ancient is idealized, the ancestors were better, the descendants have declined.

Yet in Eliot and to some extent in Pound a certain norm is placed in the past, the model of time is regressive, the future does not promise anything good. The case is quite different with Oscar Milosz. For him, no return to the old way of feeling is possible through an act of choice, and the "deviation" of poetry remains incurable until a great scientific and social transformation calls a new poetry to life; otherwise such a transformation will not occur and catastrophe will befall all mankind. His model of time is thus progressive and his eyes are turned to the future with hope or fear, which confirms his chosen affinity with the late eighteenth and early nineteenth centuries.

Fear of the future was not unknown to Milosz. While *A Few Words on Poetry* announces a great renewal, its last passage admits the possibility of a different outcome.

> It is possible that none of this will happen and that the little emaciated poetry of today is just a driveling of final exhaustion and senility. But that would be a sign not of drying up of art but of the end of humanity. Who knows? Perhaps we are much older, much more blasé, much further from God than we think, than Plato's Timaeus thought himself. If it is so, nothing is left us except to wish that at least a new Ezekiel will appear and that he will know as well as the ancient one how to shout amid light-

nings: An end! The end has come upon the four corners of the land! Now is the end come upon thee!

At the beginning of the text under discussion we read an enigmatic sentence: poetry "appears to us as bound, more rigorously than any other mode of expression, to the spiritual and physical Movement of which it is a generator and a guide." It is worth nothing that it is not the word Progress but Movement (capitalized) that is used, and this has manifold implications, for Progress denotes a linear ascension while Movement stresses incessant change and a dialectical play of opposites. By its nature poetry engenders Movement, change, and may even be found at the origin of scientific discoveries, if not directly then through osmosis. It also functions as a "guide" to Movement, and this we may interpret to mean that the language of every historical period receives its definite shape through poetry.

Because human reality is conceived as subject to incessant movement, to changeability, Oscar Milosz in his formulations seems closer to such poets as Bertolt Brecht and Pablo Neruda than to the modern scoffers for whom the structure of society, as it now exists, is opaque but stable. I suspect that his writings, as well as my conversations with him, helped me to elaborate a certain method, for a long time unconscious, of assimilating Marxism. It was based upon the conviction that the Marxists touched the most essential problems of our century, which is why one should not bypass their theories with indifference. One should not, however, trust them too much, for often they draw the wrong conclusions from the correct premises, always yielding to the pressure of their own doctrines and bending the facts to them. In any case a misunderstanding is possible here: if it is true that in my youth I sympathized with the left, then how could I be influenced at the same time by a mystic, to use a label often applied to my cousin? In the thirties, that seemed to be a serious contradiction. Now, with the perspective of time, I see no contradiction at all.

In 1931, in the city of Wilno, a literary group, Żagary, was created and I was one of its founders. This occurred shortly after the crash of the American stock market in 1929, which had enormous consequences not only in the United States. Unemployment was rising in European countries and reached 8 million in Germany; only a revolution seemed able to save the world from starvation and war, now that capitalism had entered the phase of decline. Unfortunately, the revolution prepared in neighboring Germany was to be a National Socialist one. The second adjective indicated a concession to the faith in socialism widespread among German workers, just as the presence of Karl Marx's thought was to dictate the inscription on the gates of Auschwitz: "Arbeit macht frei." No wonder that in such an atmosphere our group was on the left. Yet, strangely enough, waiting for the revolution did not prevent us from also expecting an apocalyptic catastrophe: this was more an intuitive foreboding than anything else, for even the generalized brutality and Hitler's attempts to seize power could not have foretold what was to come; horror was simply in the air. Our group was given the name of "catastrophists," which makes me reflect on the various forms taken by "the principle of hope," to use Ernst Bloch's expression. The principle of hope points to the romantic origin of Marxism, for, after all, Marx's philosophy took shape in the Age of Raptures and the date of the Communist Manifesto, 1848, is itself sufficiently eloquent. The principle of hope is also operative whenever people foresee a cataclysm that will put an end to the established order so that a new, purified reality can appear—purified by a revolution, by a flood, or by a "conflagration universelle." In other words, there is no great contradiction between joyous and fearful expectations. This can be demonstrated by the example of Dostoevsky, a writer formed by both the Age of Reason and the Age of Raptures. In his mature years he believed in the coming end of the world, in the Star Wormwood of the Apocalypse. Yet he remained faithful to his socialist youth, for he continued to search for an ideal society in which everyone would, of his own accord, renounce his ego for the sake of the community, except that now this Kingdom of God on earth was to arrive at the very end or after the end of human history. I think that similarly, in our group of "catastrophists," the two meanings of hope were interlaced and merged with each other.

Is poetry possible if it isolates itself from the Movement which was of such importance to Oscar Milosz? Formulated differently, the question reads: is noneschatological poetry possible? That would be a poetry indifferent to the existence of the Past-Future axis and to the "last things"—Salvation and Damnation, Judgment, the Kingdom of God, the goal of History—in other words, to everything that connects the time assigned to one human life with the time of all humanity. It is difficult to answer the question. Old Chinese poetry seems to have been like that, but we may be falling victim to an illusion by dealing too superficially with a civilization many of whose complexities are inaccessible to us. In our civilization, characterized by Daniel Halévy as subject to "l'accélération de l'histoire," a link between poetry and Movement is probably inevitable, and hope, conscious or unconscious, is what sustains the poet. It is possible that the gloom of twentieth-century poetry can be explained by the pattern that resulted from the "schism and misunderstanding between the poet and the great human family." This goes against the grain of our civilization, shaped as it is by the Bible and, for that reason, eschatological to the core.

3
The Lesson of Biology

MUCH has been written on the poet as a person who differs from others in that his childhood does not end and who preserves in himself something of the child throughout his life. This is true to a large extent, at least in the sense that his childhood perceptions have great durability and his first poems, half-childish, already bear some traits of his subsequent oeuvre. After all, the moments of happiness or of horror experienced by a child determine the personality of the adult. But the thought of a poet also depends upon what he learns about the world from his parents and teachers.

We should remember how many years of our lives are spent in school. There and nowhere else are we prepared to participate in our civilization. In school we are indoctrinated every day, until our notions do not differ from those of our contemporaries and we dare not doubt certain axioms, for instance, that the Earth revolves around the sun. Varying political systems have their own forms of indoctrination, but since the entire planet has fallen sway to the cult of science which arose in the sixteenth and seventeenth centuries on a small patch of Western Europe, a Chinese, American, or Russian child receives in a diluted and vulgarized form the same knowledge, based upon the discoveries of Copernicus, Newton, and Darwin. It is rather difficult to comprehend all the strangeness of that transformation: the total defeat of images of the world which might be able to compete with those imposed by science, and hence the defeat of all non-Western ways of thinking. Only the mind of a paradoxalist, like that of the Russian philosopher Lev Shestov, is capable of giving us a moment of meditation on how the upbringing of a young savage who believed in ghosts and magic differed from that of a modern child. Shestov wrote this at the very beginning of the twentieth century:

> It is another matter with a child of our society: his mind is unencumbered by fairy tales; he knows that demons and sorcerers do not exist, and he trains his mind not to believe such lies, even if his heart is inclined toward the miraculous. But, on the other hand, from a very early age, he is given reliable information, the implausibility of which surpasses absolutely every fib ever told by the most imaginative writers of fairy tales. For example, he is told—and in an authoritative tone before which all doubt subsides and must subside—that the Earth is not motionless, as the evidence indicates, that the Sun does not revolve around the Earth, that the sky is not a solid, that the horizon is only an optical illusion and so on.

In that manner, according to Shestov, there arises "a tendency in each of us to accept as truth only that which to our entire being seems false."

Without much exaggeration it can be said that poetry, for the majority of poets, is a continuation of their school notebooks or is, both literally and figuratively, written on their margins. Notions of geography, history, or physics encountered for the first time, and for that reason particularly vivid, provide the background for many renowned poems, as for instance Rimbaud's *Le Bateau ivre*. Besides, the importance of the particular subjects taught is constantly changing. In Rimbaud's time geography and history were still the leading subjects, but were increasingly yielding to the natural sciences and primarily to biology.

The adversaries of the theory of evolution, invoking its conflict with the Bible, appraised the danger correctly, for the imagination, once visited by the images of the evolutionary chain, is lost to certain varieties of religious belief. Copernicus' discovery deprived the Earth of its central place in the universe, but the discovery of man's animal origins was no less a shock. Not only because the very singularity of being human was brought into question, but also because the attack was aimed indirectly at the meaning of human death. Nature in its incredible prodigality, producing the billions of creatures necessary to maintain the species, is absolutely indifferent to the fate of the individual. Once integrated into Nature, man also changes into a statistical cipher and becomes expendable. This erosion touches every human being's perception of life in terms of salvation and damnation. It is as if one image of life, the traditional image, were covered by another one, the scientific, thus producing the constant anxiety that arises when the mind cannot cope with contradictions and reproaches itself for inconsistency. At school, contradictions are perpetuated by such subjects as literature and history, where a certain coded system of values persists, values difficult to reconcile with scientific objectivism. As to poetry, it must shift for itself as best it can in the new conditions where imagination is losing its foundation, that is, its vision of the central place of man, and of any given individual, in space and time. Modern poetry has responded to this situation with various tactics, and perhaps their history will be written one day. Were I to undertake that project (and I have no such intention), I would examine the school curricula of several decades, knowing in advance that I would discover an increasing dose of biology at the expense of the humanities, languages, and history; then I would look for some correlation between science-oriented education and the philosophy manifesting itself in poems. It seems to me that in such a test American schools and American poetry would prove the most informed by science. But other countries would not be far behind.

I am going to quote now a poem that is a good example of the influence exerted by the lessons of biology. I must briefly explain why I chose this poem, since I could have chosen others, equally useful for my purposes, which I would not have had to present, as I do this one, in translation. Poland is a country of numerous women poets. In the sixties I noticed the poems of a very young poet, Halina Poświatowska. They had a poignant tone, a despair at the mortality of the flesh, at being totally enclosed in that mortal flesh, and hence a particularly strong perception of love as constantly menaced, on the border of nonbeing. I learned that this young woman had a serious heart condition. In the seventies, when she died having barely reached thirty, a group of her friends tried to preserve her legend. At that time a well-known woman poet, Wisława Szymborska, dedicated a poem to her memory. Its title, "Autotomy," taken from zoology textbooks, means self-section. The creature that appears in it, the holothurian, also bears the name of sea cucumber.

AUTOTOMY

In danger, the holothurian splits itself in two:
it offers one self to be devoured by the world
and, in its second self, escapes.

Violently it divides itself into a doom and a salvation,
into a penalty and a recompense, into what was and what
will be.

In the middle of the holothurian's body a chasm opens
and its edges immediately become alien to each other.

On the one edge, death, on the other, life.
Here despair, there hope.

If there is a balance, the scales do not move.
If there is justice, here it is.

To die as much as necessary, without overstepping the bounds.
To grow again from a salvaged remnant.

We, too, know how to split ourselves
but only into the flesh and a broken whisper.
Into the flesh and poetry.

On one side the throat, on the other, laughter,
slight, quickly dying down.

Here a heavy heart, there *non omnis moriar*,
Three little words, like three little plumes of light.

We are not cut in two by a chasm.
A chasm surrounds us.

Once, a long time ago, another observation of nature, commonplace and not scientific, provided philosophers and poets with a metaphor for the passage from life to death. It was the observation of the transformation undergone by a pupa when it changes into a butterfly, of a body being left behind by a soul liberating itself. That dualism of the soul and the body accompanied our civilization through several centuries. It does not, however, exist in the poem I quoted. A chasm opens in the flesh of the holothurian, a division into two corporal "selves" occurs. Beginning with the Renaissance, another kind of dualism was added to the dualism of soul and body. That was, as George Steiner has also pointed out, the dualism of fame and oblivion, expressed by the maxim *ars longa, vita brevis* and by that great incitement to make one's name live in the memory of posterity: not everything dies, *non omnis moriar*. This might be called additional insurance, running parallel to the Christian one; moreover, such strivings were in harmony with the ambiguous coexistence of the heritage of antiquity and the message of the Gospels, wherever Latin was the universal language. Of course, only a few could secure fame for themselves, and thus the maxim about the shortness of life and the longevity of art was aristocratic. Besides, the stress was on social reception, on renown, not on the work itself. Recognition and the gratitude of posterity, even if belated and not in the poet's own lifetime, becomes one of great clichés of Western civilization. It remains valid, however, only as long as the bond uniting the poet to "the great human family" continues to exist.

Strange things happen in the poetry of the second half of the nineteenth century: instead of stressing the longevity of art, the solitary rebels who opposed the right-thinking citizens elevated art so high as to remove from it any goals whatsoever and began to glorify it as a thing unto itself, *l'art pour l'art*. In the very midst of a universal weakening of values deprived of their metaphysical foundations, there arises the idea of a poem outside that crisis. Such a poem should be perfectly self-sufficient, submitted to its own laws, and organized as a peculiar anti-world. Now the reward is not recognition by posterity but rather the fulfillment of the poet's personality, as if he were leaving forever a cast of his own face: "Tel qu'en lui même enfin l'éternité le change" (Such as into himself at last eternity changes him), as Mallarmé says in his poem "The Tomb of Edgar Poe."

The poem by Szymborska comes long after the cult of sovereign, haughty poetry. We have been witnessing the gradual waning of that cult and, with it, the weakening of the human personality dispossessed of its uniqueness by social laws and psychological determinants, which turned it into an interchangeable statistical unit. In Szymborska we are divided not into the flesh and a surviving oeuvre but into "the flesh and a broken whisper"; poetry is no more than a broken whisper, quickly dying laughter. If not everything dies, then it remains only for a short moment, and the *non omnis moriar* of poetry acquires a rather ironic meaning.

We all participate in the transformations of the image of the world which do not depend on our will, and we try to assuage their radical impact by not thinking things through to the bitter end. Few are daring enough to make brutally simple statements. William Blake was one of the first to notice the nefarious influence of science on "the Divine Arts of Imagination" and proclaimed as enemies of what he called the Mental Gift a diabolic trinity: Bacon, Locke, and Newton. He wrote:

> The Spectre is the Reasoning Power in Man, and when separated
> From Imagination and closing itself as in steel in a ratio
> Of the things of Memory, It thence frames Laws and Moralities
> To destroy Imagination, the Divine Body, by Martyrdoms and Wars.

Far from any intention to combat science or defend any flat-earth theory, but simply to show the conflict in all its acuteness, I wish to remind you what Blake says in defense of the naive imagination:

> And every Space that a Man views around his dwelling-place
> Standing on his own roof or in his garden on a mount
> Of twenty-five cubits in height, such space is his universe.
> . . .
> As to that false appearance which appears to the reasoner
> As of a globe rolling thro' Voidness, it is a delusion of Ulro.

What was at stake, and Blake understood it well, was saving man from images of a totally "objective," cold, indifferent world, from which the Divine Imagination has been alienated. Precisely half a century after his death, this rapid erosion of belief in any world other than one submitted to a mathematical determinism appears at the center of Dostoevsky's work and Nietzsche's work. Moreover, there is a possibility that the erosion of all values that have no place in the scientific Weltanschauung will touch the very notion of truth, in other words, that its criteria will be recognized as valid only within an arbitrarily selected system of references. Anticipating this,

Nietzsche offered the following definition of the state of mind that would become common in the not too distant future, and which we can recognize in ourselves:

> What is a belief? How does it originate? Every belief is a considering-something-true.
>
> The most extreme form of nihilism would be the view that every belief, every considering-something-true, is necessarily false because there simply is no *true world*. Thus: a *perspectival appearance* whose origin lies in us (in so far as we continaully *need* a narrower, abbreviated, simplified world).*

The poem of Szymborska I just read represents a poetics that corresponds to the fluidity of all standards, now universally felt. In the repertory of the twentieth century there is no place either for a platonic dualism of soul and body or for eternal fame—that would not accord with our sensitivity to constantly changing styles and tastes—nor is there any place for a work-in-itself, that perhaps final attempt at saving some absolute criteria. What will remain after us is a broken whisper, dying laughter. And we have no right to degrade that clear and cruel consciousness, for it is not so far from a certain heroic virtue. It is hard to tell whether another of Nietzsche's prophecies is going to be fulfilled, but his words about the superhuman greatness to which man will be compelled are worth recalling:

> That is the measure of strength to what extent we can admit to ourselves, without perishing, the merely *apparent* character, the necessity of lies.
>
> To this extent nihilism, as the denial of a truthful world, of being, might be *a divine way of thinking.*

Could we without perishing withstand a situation in which the things surrounding us lose their being, where there is no

* *The Will to Power* (1887), translated by Walter Kaufmann and R. J. Hollindale (New York: Random House, 1968).

true world? Twentieth-century poetry answers that question in the negative. Its heroism is forced and offers no indication that we are on the verge of becoming superhuman. When poets discover that their words refer only to words and not to a reality which must be described as faithfully as possible, they despair. This is probably one cause of modern poetry's somber tone. In addition, poets are threatened by isolation. The bond between them and "the great human family" was still intact in the era of romanticism, that is, the Renaissance pattern of fame, gratitude from, and recognition by others was still operative. Later, when poetry moved underground and bohemia turned away with scorn from the philistines, it found serious support in the idea of a work of Art with a capital A, its absolute meaningfulness. Poetry entered the twentieth century convinced of a fundamental antagonism between Art and the world, but Art's fortress was already crumbling and the sense of the poet's superiority to ordinary mortals had begun to lose its highest justification. After all, the author of little volumes of poems incomprehensible to the public, volumes that go unread, can draw scant comfort from a belief that a book contains no more than a broken whisper and dying laughter.

The lesson of biology brought many changes in our imagination, not only those that pertain to the fate of the individual. Imperceptibly, we alter our attitude toward the great catastrophes afflicting thousands or millions of people. It is difficult to understand why the earthquake in Lisbon in 1755 had such an impact on the minds of the men of the Enlightenment and provided occasion for a key debate. The number of victims, around 60,000, is modest when compared to the figures of losses in modern wars, but also modest in comparison with the decrease of population resulting from the black death in the Middle Ages. Such calamities, however, were treated as God's dispensation. The destruction of Lisbon, on the other hand, furnished an argument to the deists who maintained that Providence was not involved in events, for God, the great clockmaker, had left the world to its own course. Otherwise, they affirmed, he should be accused of mindless cruelty. Perhaps that reasoning is a little too abstract for us, for historical tragedies of our time make us cry out in protest. *Somebody* must be responsible, but if we start to look for a reasoned explanation, no other possibility is left to us than to follow the Epicureans with their contention that gods are either omnipotent but not good or good but not omnipotent. Nevertheless, the lesson of biology means a triumph of the scientific Weltanschauung, according to which only the chain of causes and effects is responsible. A transfer of that line of thought from the domain of nature into the domain of the social, whether justified or not, then appears obvious. Of course, it would be senseless to accuse science of having practical effects that differ from the scientists' original intentions. Yet we should realize that science not only contributes to the perfecting of ever more lethal means of conducting war. It also penetrates the very fabric of collective life, causing transformations whose range still eludes our comprehension. The pollution of the mind by certain images, those side effects of science, is analogous to the pollution of the natural surroundings by technology derived from the same science. Thus, for instance, "the survival of the fittest" in its vulgarized form prompted naturalism in literature but also created the climate for exterminating millions of human beings in the name of a presumed social hygiene. At the same time, it was science that provided the techniques for genocide, just as a little earlier it had provided the instruments for massacre in trench warfare.

In the twentieth century, as never before, poets were forced to resist such a pressure of facts that ran contrary to their somewhat childish nature. Early on, in the first years of life, every one of us must, on our own, discover the harsh laws of existence contrary to our desires. A flame, so lovely to look at, burns the fingers when grasped; a glass tossed from the table does not stay in the air but falls and breaks to pieces. The desire for the miraculous is exposed to severe trials by the so-called natural order of things, into which gradually we are introduced by our family and school, as a preparation for life in society. It is possible that poets are particularly recalcitrant to that training, and that is why they become the voice of the universal human longing for liberation from what is cold as two times two is four, harsh and pitiless. For a long time certain zones of reality were excluded by religion from the power of blind laws, and perhaps for that reason there was something of an alliance between religion and poetry. Not only was the fate of cities and nations included in that category, but the fate of mankind as a whole. The deists' argument after the destruction of Lisbon by earthquake did not, after all, succeed in abolishing a well-rooted faith in Providence. The whole Age of Raptures was full of messianic dreams about the peculiar calling of one nation or of given nations, a calling written down in advance in God's book. But also later, in the age of steam and electricity, the notion of Progress bore all the traits of a providential arrangement that prepared the paths mankind would take.

An important difference between the nineteenth and the twentieth centuries probably derives from the crossing of a certain threshold: things too atrocious to think of did not seem possible. But, beginning in 1914, they proved to be more and more possible. A discovery has been made, that "civilizations are mortal." Thus there is nothing to protect Western civilization from plunging into chaos and barbarity. The state of savagery, which seemed to belong to the remote past, returned as the tribal rituals of totalitarian states. The extermination camp became a central fact of the century and barbed wire its emblem. Thomas Mann was undoubtedly right in seeing Joseph Conrad's *Heart of Darkness* as a work inaugurating the twentieth century. Europeans had for a long time been effectively hiding certain horrors in their colonial backyard, until they were visited by them with a vengeance. It was precisely in Europe that countries were divided up between the superpowers as if it were a question of distributing riches or herds of cattle, though what was at stake were people, their cities, and homelands. An escalation of danger occurred too, for atomic weapons brought about the probability of the improbable, the destruction of the Earth. Like a child who finds out that fire burns fingers and that the sharp edge of a table if struck causes pain, mankind encountered naked data that were connected according to the law of cause and effect, and without any divine protection now to guarantee a favorable outcome.

Thinking about man in naturalistic terms was furthered by statistics on the rapid population increase on planet Earth. The conversation I am about to relate would never have been possible before this century. It took place in Warsaw during the last world war, under the German occupation, between me and an intellectual, a member of the Communist underground. I expressed my doubts as to his "either-or" premise, for in his opinion whoever wanted to resist Nazism effectively had no other choice than to accept the Soviet system completely. My reservations concerned the mass terror practiced by the Soviet dictator. My interlocutor shrugged and replied: "A million people more, a million people less, what's the difference?"

True, what is the difference? That voice of protest we hear in ourselves when we learn of places where human beings torture other human beings resounds in a void and has no justification other than itself. While the millions of men, women, and children who died in the years 1939–1945 are still being mourned, it is difficult not to think about the tendency, stronger every day, to equate human beings with flies or cockroaches; we may assume that some properly sublime goal could provide reasons for exterminating flies, while those who were left in peace would remain perfectly indifferent.

A twentieth-century poet is like a child trained to respect the naked facts by adults who, in turn, were initiated in an exceptionally cruel manner. He would like to base his yes and no on some foundation, but to do that he would have to admit that behind the interplay of phenomena there is a meaningful world structure to which our hearts and minds are allied. Everything, however, conspires to destroy that supposition, as if it were a remnant of our faith in the miraculous. Does this mean that by taking science for its guide the human species is now reaching maturity? That is possible. But there is another possibility. The social fabric assimilates the side effects of science with a certain lag, so that the notions and images born out of nineteenth-century science have only now just reached it. A new image of the world, still timidly developing, the one in which the miraculous has a legitimate place, has had no time to be widely recognized.

If this is so, the twentieth century is a purgatory in which the imagination must manage without the relief that satisfies one of the essential needs of the human heart, the need for protection. Existence appears as ruled by necessity and chance, with no divine intervention; until recently God's hand used to bring help to pious rulers and to punish sinful rulers. But now even the idea of Progress, which was nothing else but Providence secularized, no longer provides any guarantee. Poets, always inclined by the nature of their art to distribute praise and blame, stand before a mechanism submitted to the actions of blind force and must suspend their yes and no in midair. No wonder then that some people search for guides whose thought could cope with great reduction, but who at the same time would offer a new opening and a new hope. Our century produced a few eminent thinkers whose importance has been growing with every decade, and by mentioning one of them here, Simone Weil, I succumb to an autobiographic temptation (though I am no longer isolated in my respect for that writer).

"God consigned all phenomena without exception to the mechanism of the world"; "necessity is the veil of God": this is

Simone Weil. She extended determinism to all phenomena, including the psychological. For her this was the domain of what she used to call *la pesanteur*, gravity. At the same time, she believed that whoever asks for bread will not receive stones, for there is another domain, that of Grace. The parallel existence of these two domains goes to the very core of her philosophy, which legitimizes contradiction when no solution is possible; in this case, there is no insoluble contradiction between divine intervention and universal necessity. Since I am concerned here with the fate of poetry, I would like to recall one of Simone Weil's texts that pertains directly to literature. This is a letter to the editor of *Cahiers du Sud* apparently written in the summer of 1941, under the impact of the fall of France:

> I believe that writers of the period which just ended are responsible for the miseries of our time. By this I mean not only the defeat of France; the miseries of our time go much further. They spread all over the world, i.e., Europe, America and other continents to the extent they have felt the Western influence. . . .
>
> An essential feature of the first half of the twentieth century consists in the weakening and near disappearance of the notion of value. This is one of those rare phenomena which seem to be really new in the history of mankind. Of course it is possible that such a phenomenon existed in periods which subsequently have fallen into oblivion, just as will perhaps be the case of our epoch. That phenomenon manifested itself in many fields alien to literature, and even in all fields. It might be observed in the substitution of quantity for quality in industrial production, in the substitution of diplomas for general culture among students. Science itself no longer possessed a criterion of value after science in the classical sense came to an end. But writers were by nature of their profession guardians of a treasure now lost, while some of them take pride in that loss.

To quote Simone Weil is, I realize, a dangerous endeavor. Her thought goes against mental habits which are taken for granted, and the notions she uses, such as good and evil, may easily cause a person who quotes her to be labeled a reactionary. Yet I guess I must agree with Simone Weil's opinion on certain trends in art and literature, such as dadaism and surrealism. They are highly regarded in the artistic chronicle of our century, and her scornful rejection of them may provoke protest:

> Dadaism, surrealism are extreme cases. They expressed the frenzy of total license, the frenzy which takes hold of the mind when, rejecting all consideration of value, it plunges into the immediate. Good is a pole that by necessity attracts the human mind, not only in action but in every effort, including the effort of pure intelligence. The surrealists set up a model of non-oriented thought; they chose for a supreme value a total absence of value. License has always entranced men and that is why, throughout history, cities have been sacked. But the sacking of cities has not always had its equivalent in literature. Surrealism is such an equivalent.

I anticipate the objection that it was the defeat of France that prompted Simone Weil to pronounce such bitter accusations. Let us consider, though, that the defeat in question was a classic case of the weakening of resistance against totalitarianism and that the dadaists and surrealists had nothing but scorn for democracy, in which, they were the worthy successors of bohemia. Who knows, perhaps a denial of a truthful way of thinking, is attended indirectly by serious political consequences, though those consequences may appear in circumstances not necessarily the same as those in France during World War II. Behind the historical occasion of the criticism Simone Weil makes of surrealism, we may find content still relevant for us today, especially in the following passage from her letter:

> Other writers of the same period and of the preceding period did not go so far, but all of them—with three or four exceptions

perhaps—were marked by the same deficiency, a deficiency in their sense of value. Such words as spontaneity, sincerity, gratuitousness, richness, enrichment, words which imply a nearly complete indifference to oppositions of values, appeared more often from their pen than words which are related to good and evil. Besides, the latter type of words suffered a degradation, particularly those related to good, as Valéry noticed a few years ago.

Simone Weil was courageous. If she considered something true, she would say it, without fear of being labeled. In fact, she might have been suspected of entering into an alliance with the reactionaries, for in our century it is they who are the rear guard defending a discrimination among values. The poet of today, enmeshed in various professional rituals, is too ashamed to attain such frankness. Of what is he ashamed? Of the child in himself who wants the earth to be flat, enclosed beneath the cupola of the sky, and who wants pairs of clearly drawn opposites to exist: truth and falsity, good and evil, beauty and ugliness. Unfortunately, he was taught in school that this is a naive image of the world and belongs to the past. All that remains for him is to employ defensive tactics, to try to organize his own subjective space without having any certainty except that he is like the holothurian in Szymborska's poem, which divides itself into a body and a broken whisper.

My assessment sounds fatalistic and that makes me uneasy, for I have much hope and I should after all attempt to show it in some way. First, I have defined poetry as a "passionate pursuit of the Real," and undoubtedly it is that; no science or philosophy can change the fact that a poet stands before reality that is every day new, miraculously complex, inexhaustible, and tries to enclose as much of it as possible in words. That elementary contact, verifiable by the five senses, is more important than any mental construction. The never-fulfilled desire to achieve a mimesis, to be faithful to a detail, makes for the health of poetry and gives it a chance to survive periods unpropitious to it. The very act of naming things presupposes a faith in their existence and thus in a true world, whatever Nietzsche might say. Of course there are poets who only relate words to words, not to their models in things, but their artistic defeat indicates that they are breaking some sort of rule of poetry.

Second, the historical force which carries us is as much constructive as destructive, for it is inventing means against destruction. It would be vain to dream of an earth purged of science and technology. On the contrary, only the further development of science and technology can prevent the pollution of the natural environment and save the inhabitants of the planet from starvation. It is much the same thing with the vulgarized scientific Weltanschauung propagated by the schools. The analogy is not perfect, since it is much more difficult to imagine the means able to counter an already universalized way of thinking than to devise measures against the pollution of rivers and lakes. Nevertheless, there are signs that allow us to expect a basic transformation at the very source, which means that technological civilization may begin to see reality as a labyrinth of mirrors, no less magical than the labyrinth seen by alchemists and poets. That would be a victory for William Blake and his "Divine Arts of Imagination"—but also for the child in the poet, a child too long trained by adults.

4
A Quarrel with Classicism

IN THE 1980s Poland, if not for its sad political circumstances, could be commemorating the anniversary of its first great poet, Jan Kochanowski. In fact two anniversaries, the 450th anniversary of his birth (he was born in 1530) and the 400th anniversary of his death (he died in 1584). I introduce him here not only because I apprenticed with him, as does every Polish poet, but also because, by reflecting on what we today call a Renaissance poet, we can approach some of the more irksome problems of the twentieth century.

For all Europe the Renaissance was the hour of Italy, and Kochanowski spent several years there, traveling, studying Latin and Greek authors in Padua, writing poems in Latin. He did not switch to the vernacular immediately. That seems to have occurred in Paris where he found himself on a return journey from Italy to Poland, and where he was perhaps prompted to rivalry by the example of Ronsard, who wrote in his native French, not in Latin. Kochanowski's first Polish work, a hymn of gratitude addressed to God, "What do you want from us, Lord, for your bounteous gifts," strikes us by its formal perfection and, in addition, is characteristic of a poet who, in an era of interdenominational strife, managed to preserve a skeptical distance from both the Catholic camp and the Reformation.

The Polish literary language achieved maturity over a few decades in the sixteenth century and, as I said in my first chapter, has not changed as much as English has since the time of Edmund Spenser, let alone Chaucer. This means that readers of Kochanowski assimilate him linguistically as they would a contemporary poet, but at the same time feel that they themselves belong to a completely different period and realize that many changes have occurred in the place and function of poetry, especially during the last one hundred years. This raises questions for anyone who attempts to see whether that old poetry really appeals to him or whether he is just paying homage to values that are, for the most part, museum pieces.

Kochanowski's artistic achievement is unquestionable, which lends this problem particular importance. He was not only a talented but a well-educated poet, as was proper for a man of the Renaissance. Wiktor Weintraub, who has devoted several studies to Kochanowski,* proved that his familiarity with Greek poets, read in the original (and that was not common even among the elite), assured Kochanowski a significant degree of independence from Latin models, namely from Horace and Seneca. The choice of one or another such master, however, does not change the fact that he drew his models from antiquity, in which he resembled the poets of La Pléiade; were I a Frenchman, I would be writing about the readers of Ronsard or of Joachim du Bellay.

What we are dealing with here is simply the poetics of classicism, alien to a poet of today but also intriguing in their strangeness. In his famous work *Mimesis* Erich Auerbach pointed to a certain lack of reality wherever a convention is used: where the poet creates as beautiful a structure as possible out of topoi universally known and fixed, instead of trying

* Gathered in the volume *Rzecz Czarnoleska* (Krakow: Wydawnictwo Literackie, 1977).

to name what is real and yet unnamed. Thus the literary conventions which bind author and reader form a barrier, and it is difficult to step beyond it into chaotic reality with its inexhaustible richness of detail. In antiquity, Auerbach writes, "the question of style became really acute when the spread of Christianity exposed Holy Scripture, and Christian literature in general, to the aesthetic criticism of highly educated pagans. They were horrified at the claim that the highest truths were contained in writings composed in a language to their minds impossibly uncivilized and in total ignorance of stylistic categories." But it is precisely for this reason that we learn more of everyday life in the Roman Empire from the Gospels than from the Latin poetry of the Golden Age. Horace and Vergil so filter and distill their material that we can only guess at some of the down-to-earth data hidden behind their lines.

A similar distillation also appears in Kochanowski. For a poet of his time he is earthy enough to teach us a good deal about the mores common to his gentry milieu. That, however, applies to his short epigrams called in the Italian manner *fraszki* (from *frasca*, a twig) or to his journalism in verse, which is not among his highest achievements. As to his lyrical poetry, it organized the language excellently but is composed of topoi, either religious or expressing the Horatian *carpe diem*. An exception is *Laments*, a cycle of nineteen poems written after the death of his small daughter Ursula, where he breaks the convention forbidding the expression of *real* pain in a work of that type. This brought some discomfort to Kochanowski's contemporaries but, thanks to that personal element, the *Laments* are still moving even though four centuries have passed since they were written.

In order to illustrate how we differ from poets of the sixteenth century, I will quote a short fragment from Kochanowski's play in verse entitled *The Dismissal of the Grecian Envoys*. The subject is taken from a few lines of *The Iliad* and from the rich literature that grew up around that epic. Before the outbreak of the Trojan War, Greek envoys arrive in Troy to demand that Helen be delivered to them. The fate of the city is at stake. What is better: to deliver Helen and have peace, or to keep her and have war? In our century the same moment of decision was chosen as a subject by Giraudoux: shortly before the outbreak of World War II his play *La Guerre de Troie n'aura pas lieu* was performed in Paris (its English version bears the title *Tiger at the Gate*). One of the most moving passages in Kochanowski's play is Cassandra's complaint. Here are its opening lines:

> Why vainly does thou torture me, Apollo?
> Who, when thou lent'st me power of prophecy,
> Gav'st to my words no weight! Unto the winds
> Fly all my prophecies, gaining with men
> Credence accorded dreams and idle tales.
> My fettered heart, my loss of memory
> Whom will they aid? To whom is profitable
> This alien spirit, speaking through my lips,
> And all my thoughts, ruled over by a guest
> Grievous, unbearable? In vain do I
> Resist! I suffer violence; I rule
> Myself no longer; I am not my own.*

Let us note a certain mutual understanding between the poet and his public. He assumes, and in this he is not mistaken, that everybody knows the story of the king of Troy's daughter, Cassandra, who rejected Apollo's amorous advances and, as her punishment, received from him the gift of seeing the future, a punishment, for no one takes her prophecies seriously. In Kochanowski's play it is assumed that the refusal to deliver Helen to the Greeks means war and that Troy will be destroyed; therefore Cassandra tells the truth. The situation is thus defined in advance, and the audience expects no sur-

* Translated by Ruth Earl Merrill in *Poems* by Jan Kochanowski (Berkeley: University of California Press, 1928; New York: AMS Press, 1978).

prises from the poet, since it knows from *The Iliad* what occurs after the curtain goes down. The audience expects only good poetic craft in a work on a given topic.

A given topic, and topoi polished by long use like pebbles in a stream: that's what both fascinates and irritates twentieth-century poets. For us classicism is a paradise lost, for it implies a community of beliefs and feelings which unite poet and audience. No doubt the poet was not then separated from the "human family," though obviously that was a family of a modest size since the illiterate rural population, comprising the vast majority of the inhabitants of Poland and Europe as a whole, was perfectly indifferent to that system of allusions to Homer and Horace. But even if we take the small number into account, there was still a sense of belonging—thus a situation radically different from the loneliness of the bohemians, who could at best find readers among their peers and whose descendant and heir is the poet of today. Perhaps there is a good craftsman concealed in every poet who dreams about a material already ordered, with ready-made comparisons and metaphors endowed with nearly archetypal effectiveness and, for that reason, universally accepted; what remains then is to work on chiseling the language. Were classicism only a thing of the past, none of this would merit attention. In fact, it constantly returns as a temptation to surrender to merely graceful writing. For, after all, one can reason as follows: all attempts at enclosing the world in words are and will be futile; there is a basic incompatibility between language and reality, as demonstrated by the desperate pursuit practiced by those who wanted to capture it even through "le dérèglement de tous sens" or by the use of drugs. If this is so, then let us respect the rules of the game as adopted by consensus and appropriate to a given historical period, and let us not advance a rook as if it were a knight. In other words, let us make use of conventions, aware that they are conventions and no more than that.

Who has not felt this temptation? Yet objection comes to

mind. There is a logic to modern art, in poetry, in painting, in music, and that is the logic of incessant *movement*. We have been thrown outside the orbit of a language ordered by conventions and have been condemned to risk and danger, but because of that we remain faithful to the definition of poetry as a "passionate pursuit of the Real." Unfortunately, the weakening of faith in the existence of the objective reality situated beyond our perceptions seems to be one of the causes of the malaise so common in modern poetry, which senses something like the loss of its raison d'être.

Is there really no "true world"? We can answer as did that Greek who, upon hearing the argument of Zeno of Elea that movement is an illusion since an arrow in flight remains motionless, got up and took two steps. The twentieth century has given us a most simple touchstone for reality: physical pain. This happened because a great number of people were submitted to torments in wars and under the rule of political terror. Of course it would be an exaggeration to single out our epoch as exceptionally horrendous. People have always suffered physical pain, died of starvation, lived as slaves. Yet all that was not common knowledge as it now is because of the shrinking of our planet and because of the mass media. Educated men lived in a certain gentle zone, enclosed within boundaries that were not to be trespassed. Kochanowski, like every poet of the Renaissance, had a middling interest, at best, in the fate of the lower classes; nor would it have crossed his mind to inquire what was happening then in central Africa.

It was only in our time that men started to visualize the simultaneity of phenomena and to feel a resulting moral anxiety. We discovered a certain unpleasant truth that constantly intrudes on us, even if we would like to forget it. Mankind has always been divided by one rule into two species: *those who know and do not speak; those who speak and do not know.* This formula can be seen as an allusion to the dialectic of master and slave, for it invokes centuries of ignorance and misery among serfs, peasants, and proletarians, who alone knew the cruelty of life in all its nakedness but had to keep it to themselves. The skill of reading and writing was the privilege of the few, whose sense of life was made comfortable by power and wealth.

Those who speak and do not know. But even if they do know, they encounter an obstacle in the form of language, which tends to coagulate in one or another kind of classicism; it readily makes recourse to conventional expressions, even if they do not adhere to reality, which is always unexpected. This became evident during the last war, when people learned firsthand the horrors of the German occupation which surpassed any of their inherited notions of evil. The number of those who knew and who spoke was then quite high, and one can marvel at the profound need that forced people to record their own experience in poems, songs, and even in inscriptions on prison walls. It would seem that, considering the extraordinary scope of the genocide planned, those works, written under great emotional stress by people deprived of hope, should have broken with all conventions. But that was not the case. The language in which the victims expressed themselves contained clichés, traces of their prewar readings, and was thus basically a cultural phenomenon. That discrepancy was chosen as the subject of a dissertation at the Sorbonne by Michał Borwicz, a veteran of the Polish resistance. His book, *Les Ecrits des condamnés à mort sous l'occupation allemande (1939–1945)*,* analyzes a great number of texts gathered from several countries, but chiefly from Poland. He defines the importance of these texts as follows:

Man, pushed to the very limit of his condition, found once more in the written word a *last rampart* against the loneliness of annihilation. His words, elaborate or awkward, cadenced or disorderly, were inspired only by the will to express, to com-

* Paris: Presses Universitaires de France, 1954.

municate and to transmit the truth. They were formulated in the worst conditions possible, were spread by impoverished means and dangerous by definition. Those words were opposed to the lie fabricated and maintained by powerful groups which had gigantic technology at their disposal and who were protected by unbounded violence.

This function of the word, exceptionally important for preserving one's humanity, does not mean that man is able to speak out other than in a style he has received from others, through his upbringing and reading, even if circumstances call for a completely different, new language. Here is what Borwicz says of that:

> As to the manner of writing, we observe in general a tendency *to simplify the style.* The "novelty" of the matter finds reflection both in "small devices" of expression (metaphors, comparisons, etc.) and in the formulas of certain works, as well as in their fabric and their internal components. Those results enrich a familiar repertory, without, however, going beyond the framework of perfectly explicable changes. On the contrary, *there is not even one work deserving attention, where the author tries to express horror by going beyond the traditional communicative language or by disintegrating it.*
>
> In this context, the writings of non-professionals (beginners, non-intellectuals) are no exception. On the contrary: indulging in clichés from before the occupation is in general more conspicuous.

The only exception Borwicz sees to this rule is some of the testimonies left by children. They attain directness not by an "expressive deformation" but because of "a realism naive yet sober, and through its soberness, evocative."

I have not permitted myself to introduce into my lecture a tragic and harsh element, seemingly ill adapted to a literary discussion, to belittle the importance of such charming poets as Kochanowski or La Pléiade. Whoever invokes genocide, starvation, or the physical suffering of our fellow men in order to attack poems or paintings practices demagoguery. It is doubtful whether mankind would gain anything if poets stopped writing idyllic poems or painters stopped painting brightly colored pictures just because there is too much suffering on the earth, in the belief that there is no place for such detached occupations. No, all I want is to make clear to myself and to my listeners is that, roughly described, a quarrel exists between classicism and realism. This is a clash of two tendencies independent of the literary fashions of a given period and of the shifting meanings of those two terms. These two opposed tendencies usually also coexist within one person. It must be said that the conflict will never end and that the first tendency is always, in one variety or another, dominant, while the second is always a voice of protest. When thinking of what is beautiful in the literature and painting of the past, what we admire and what fills us with joy simply because it exists, we must wonder at the power of nonrealistic art. Mankind appears to be dreaming a fantastic dream about itself, giving ever new but always bizarre shapes to the simplest relations between people or between man and Nature. This occurs because of Form, which has its own exigencies only partially dependent upon human intentions. Form favors a penchant for the hieratic and the classical; it resists attempts to introduce realistic detail, for instance, in painting, the black top hat and the frock coat that so incensed the critics of Courbet or, in poetry, such words as "telephone" and "train." This makes for a long history of skirmishes around existing forms which are overcome but then immediately coagulate into forms just as "artificial" as the preceding ones.

The words "art" and "artificiality" are too closely related to postulate a poetry which is not dominated by form. Form dominates poetry even if the twentieth century did witness a series of artistic revolutions occasionally as extreme as the "liberated words" of Italian futurism, an attempt to liberate words from their prescribed places in syntax. At least until World War I poetry was, in the mind of the public, recognizable by columns of lines disciplined by meter and rhyme. So-called free verse won the right of citizenship only gradually. It is interesting that the United States's contribution to the history of modern poetry is considerably more substantial than one might expect, judging by its relative cultural isolation during the nineteenth century. First, Edgar Allan Poe had a strong influence on French symbolism. Then revolutions in versification were greatly indebted to Walt Whitman's poetry, which began to penetrate Europe around 1912.

A poet today is not bound by the sonnet form or subjected to the numerous rules of poetics valid for a poet of the Renaissance or the eighteenth century. It would seem that now more than ever he is free to pursue reality. This is especially so since he borrows readily from the language of the street and because the differences between literary genres are fading away: the neat division between novel, story, poetry, and essay is no longer so clearly maintained.

And yet a glass wall of conventions rises between a poet and reality, conventions never visible until they recede into the past, there to reveal their strangeness. One may also ask whether the melancholy tone of today's poetry will not be recognized at some point as the veneer of a certain mandatory style. Not unlike ancient mythology and the Trojan War for the poets of the Renaissance, a vision deprived of hope may often be just a cliché common to the poetry of our time. And other habits limit freedom of movement. When it is not the perfection of a work that is important but expression itself, "a broken whisper," everything becomes, as it has been called, écriture. At the same time, a sensitivity to the surface stimuli of each minute and hour changes that écriture into a kind of diary of a sore epidermis. To talk about anything, just to talk, becomes an operation in itself, a means of assuaging fear. It is as if the maxim "It's not we who speak the language, but the language that speaks us" were taking its revenge. For it is true that not every poet who speaks of real things necessarily gives them the tangibility indispensable to their existence in a work of art. He may as well make them unreal.

I affirm that, when writing, every poet is making a choice between the dictates of the poetic language and his fidelity to the real. If I cross out a word and replace it with another, because in that way the line as a whole acquires more conciseness, I follow the practice of the classics. If, however, I cross out a word because it does not convey an observed detail, I lean toward realism. Yet those two operations cannot be neatly separated, they are interlocked. In addition, during these constant clashes between the two principles, a poet discovers a secret, namely that he can be faithful to real things only by arranging them hierarchically. Otherwise, as often occurs in contemporary prose-poetry, one finds a "heap of broken images, where the sun beats," fragments enjoying perfect equality and hinting at the reluctance of the poet to make a choice.

In this respect, the poet of the twentieth century can learn much from the prose writers of the past, and probably the most from Dostoevsky. His realism consisted in the reading of signs: an item in a newspaper, an overheard conversation, a popular book, a slogan, gave him access to a zone hidden from the eyes of his contemporaries. For him reality was multilayered, but not all of its layers provided clues. Dostoevsky's creative effort tended toward greater and greater hierarchization, as he attempted to capture what was essential in the spiritual adventures of the Russian intelligentsia, without being led astray by a tangled multitude of trends. He was helped in this by his strong conviction that a purely historical dimension does not exist because it is at the same time a metaphysical dimension. For him, there was a metaphysical warp and woof in the very fabric of history.

However, in spite of the blurred line between literary

genres, so that poetry and prose are no longer clearly distinguishable, a poet does not have hundreds of pages at his disposal to present his argument. The hierarchization of which I am speaking must be much more condensed, though always present as an ordering principle.

Now, as I approach the end of my lecture, I will allow myself to make a confession that will confirm what I said of classicist and realistic tendencies residing in one person and struggling with each other. Actually that confession has already been made and exists in the form of a poem I wrote over twenty years ago.

NO MORE*

I should relate sometime how I changed
My views on poetry, and how it came to be
That I consider myself today one of the many
Merchants and artisans of Old Japan,
Who arranged verses about cherry blossoms,
Chrysanthemums and the full moon.

If only I could describe the courtesans of Venice
As in a loggia they teased a peacock with a twig,
And out of brocade, the pearls of their belt,
Set free heavy breast and the reddish weal
Where the buttoned dress marked the belly,
As vividly as seen by the skipper of galleons
Who landed that morning with a cargo of gold;
And if I could find for their miserable bones
In a graveyard whose gates are licked by greasy water
A word more enduring than their last-used comb
That in the rot under tombstones, alone, awaits the light,

Then I wouldn't doubt. Out of reluctant matter
What can be gathered? Nothing, beauty at best.
And so, cherry blossoms must suffice for us
And chrysanthemums and the full moon.

It seems to me that the poem is quite perverse. We are used to viewing Chinese and Japanese poetry as examples of a pe-

* Translated by Anthony Milosz.

culiar attachment to conventions. Thus the persona speaking
here renounces his ambitious pursuit of reality and chooses
instead cherry blossoms, chrysanthemums, and the full moon;
those are permanent accessories of the kind of poetry that is
not unlike a societal game, for it is universally practiced and
assessed according to one's skill in the use of those accessories. "Merchants and artisans of Old Japan," average people
who practiced poetry in their free moments, are introduced in
order to stress the integral place of the versifier's craft in the
habits of all society. We have here a radical renouncement of
the heritage of bohemia, with its pride in the isolated and
alienated poet. And yet the speaker affirms that his choice is
an act of resignation, made because the achievement of certain
goals was for him impossible. "If only I could," he says. Could
what? Describe. Then follows a description of Venetian courtesans, which paradoxically shows us the poet achieving what,
in his opinion, was beyond his power. Yet, since this entire
image is in the conditional and has to serve as a proof of the
insufficiency of words, it is not a description which would satisfy the poet and is at best an outline, a project. Beyond the
words used, a presence is felt, of entire human lives condensed: those courtesans at the moment they receive a skipper
of galleons, their fate, imaginable but not told, their death,
their last-used comb. The real is simply too abundant; it wants
to be named, but names cannot embrace it and it remains no
more than a catalogue of data devoid of any ultimate meaning.

An author is not the best interpreter of his poems, but since
I have taken on that role I will say that I see rather serious
philosophical implications in this longing for perfect mimesis.
First, the whole great quarrel about the existence of the world
beyond our perceptions, a quarrel started by Descartes, is, so
to speak, treated parenthetically and does not interest the poet
speaking in my poem. The world exists objectively, despite
the shapes in which it appears in the mind and despite the
colors, bright or dark, lent it by the happiness or misfortune of
a particular man. That objective world can be seen as it is; yet

we may surmise that it can be seen with perfect impartiality only by God. Intent on representing it, the poet is left with the bitter realization of the inadequacy of language. Second, to desire ardently to possess an object cannot be called anything but love. The poet therefore appears as a man in love with the world, but he is condemned to eternal insatiability because he wants his words to penetrate the very core of reality. He hopes constantly and is constantly rejected. Philosophically, this is very close to the discourse on love in the *Symposium* of Plato. From the text of the poem I have just read it follows that every poet is a servant of Eros who "interprets between gods and men, conveying and talking across to the gods the prayers and sacrifices of men, and to men the commands and replies of the gods; he is the mediator who spans the chasm which divides them, and therefore in him all is bound together, and through him the arts of the prophet and the priest, their sacrifices and mysteries and charms, and all prophecy and incantation, find their way."*

It would seem that the description of Venetian courtesans provides a valid proof of language's capacity to encounter the world. But immediately the speaker undermines that conclusion. This he does most obviously by referring to a painting by Carpaccio, which depicts a yard in Venice where the courtesans are sitting and teasing a peacock with a twig. Thus not only language changes reality into a catalogue of data, but reality appears as mediated by a work of painting—in other words, not in its original state but already well ordered, already a part of culture. If reality exists, then how are we to dream of reaching it without intermediaries of one or another sort, whether they are other literary works or visions provided by the whole past of art? Thus the protest against conventions, instead of taking us to some free space where a poet can encounter the world directly, as on the first day of Creation,

* Translated by Benjamin Jowett, *The Portable Plato* (New York: Viking Press, 1961).

again sends us back to those historical strata that already exist as form.

The description of the courtesans in my poem is placed between "If only I could describe" and "Then I wouldn't doubt." And the doubt comes from the fact that matter resists amorous possession by the word, and what can be gathered out of it is "beauty at best." If I understand the persona, with whom I am identical to a certain extent, he does not have in mind the beauty contained in Nature, in views of sky, mountains, sea, sunsets, but the beauty of form in a poem or a painting. He proclaims that this does not satisfy him, since it can be obtained only at the price of renouncing the truth, which would be tantamount to a perfect mimesis. Cherry blossoms, chrysanthemums, and the full moon are ready-made pieces serving a merchant or artisan of Old Japan to arrange beautiful forms again and again. The statement affirming that this should suffice acquires a shade of irony and is in fact a declaration of disagreement with classicism.

My aim here has been to indicate a contradiction that resides at the very foundation of the poet's endeavor. This contradiction was not clearly perceived by Kochanowski or other poets of the Renaissance. Today it is difficult to escape the awareness of an internal tension between imperatives. Such tension does not invalidate my definition of poetry as "a passionate pursuit of the Real." On the contrary, it gives it more weight.

5
Ruins and
Poetry

NOW I INTEND to speak on the experience of poetry in a strictly defined time and place. The time is 1939–1945, the place, Poland. This, I feel, will provide many of the problems already touched upon with distinct exemplification. I should remind you in advance that before World War II Polish poets did not differ much in their interests and problems from their colleagues in France or Holland. The specific features of Polish literature notwithstanding, Poland belonged to the same cultural circuit as other European countries. Thus one can say that what occurred in Poland was an encounter of an European poet with the hell of the twentieth century, not hell's first circle, but a much deeper one. This situation is something of a laboratory, in other words: it allows us to examine what happens to modern poetry in certain historical conditions.

A hierarchy of needs is built into the very fabric of reality and is revealed when a misfortune touches a human collective, whether that be war, the rule of terror, or natural catastrophe. Then to satisfy hunger is more important than finding food that suits one's taste; the simplest act of human kindness toward a fellow being acquires more importance than any refinement of the mind. The fate of a city, of a country, becomes the center of everyone's attention, and there is a sudden drop in the number of suicides committed because of disappointed love or psychological problems. A great simplification of everything occurs, and an individual asks himself why he took to heart matters that now seem to have no weight. And, evidently, people's attitude toward the language also changes. It recovers its simplest function and is again an instrument serving a purpose; no one doubts that the language must name reality, which exists objectively, massive, tangible, and terrifying in its concreteness.

In the war years, poetry was the main genre of underground literature, since a poem can be contained on a single page. Poetry was circulated in manuscript or in clandestine publications, transmitted orally or sung. An anthology entitled *Poetry of Fighting Poland* published a few years ago has 1912 pages of poems and songs, written mostly under the German occupation.* The vast majority has documentary value and, at the time, fulfilled an important function; today we would not grant them high artistic rank. Only a few show any familiarity with poetic craft. All of them, however, are characterized by that law discovered by Michał Borwicz in his book on the literature of prisons and concentration camps: they belong stylistically to the prewar period, but at the same time they try to express "the new," which cannot be grasped by any of the available notions and means of expression. This poetry is often too talkative and blatant in its calls to battle while simultaneously, on a deeper level, it behaves like a mute who tries in vain to squeeze some articulate sound out of his throat; he is desperate to speak but does not succeed in communicating anything of substance. It is only later, after the war, under the pressure of a strongly felt need to find an expression for an exceptionally trying collective experience, that Polish poetry begins to move away from the stylistic modes common to the prewar poetry of many countries.

* Warsaw: PIW, 1972.

To define in a word what had happened, one can say: disintegration. People always live within a certain order and are unable to visualize a time when that order might cease to exist. The sudden crumbling of all current notions and criteria is a rare occurrence and is characteristic only of the most stormy periods in history. Perhaps the generations of Frenchmen who lived through the revolution and the Napoleonic wars felt something similar, and perhaps too Americans from the South felt they were witness to the ruins of their entire way of life after the civil war. In general, though, the nineteenth century did not experience the rapid and violent changes of the next century, whose only possible analogy may be the time of the Peloponnesian war, as we know it from Thucydides. Nevertheless, the disintegration of which I speak had already taken place in the nineteenth century, though it was under the surface and so observed by only a few. The pact concluded between Hitler and Stalin on August 23, 1939, brought all of Europe's poisons to the surface, it opened up a Pandora's box. This was a fulfillment of things that were already prepared and only waiting to reveal themselves. It is necessary to keep in mind this peculiar logic of events in order to understand how poetry reacted. Perhaps, in proclaiming the end of European culture, Dostoevsky was, to a considerable extent, motivated by his Russian anti-Western obsession. But it was precisely in that manner that poets in Poland perceived Europe sinking in consecutive stages into inhumanity—as the end of all European culture and its disgrace.

The main reproach made to culture, a reproach at first too difficult to be formulated, then finally formulated, was that it maintained a network of meanings and symbols as a facade to hide the genocide under way. By the same token, religion, philosophy, and art became suspect as accomplices in deceiving man with lofty ideas, in order to veil the truth of existence. Only the biological seemed true, and everything was reduced to a struggle within the species, and to the survival of the fittest. Yes, but that reduction had already been made. A whole system of values had been destroyed, with its neat division into good and evil, beauty and ugliness, including as well the very notion of truth. Therefore Nietzsche was not entirely mistaken in announcing "European nihilism." Yet the facade was maintained, and it provoked angry reproaches: "You spoke of the dignity of man, a being created in the image and likeness of God, of good and beauty, and look what happened; you should be ashamed of your lies." Mistrust and mockery were directed against the whole heritage of European culture. This is why many years after the war a play by Stanisław Wyspiański, *Akropolis*, written in 1904, was staged by Jerzy Grotowski in such a peculiar fashion. The play is composed of scenes from Homer and the Bible and thus sums up the main components of Western culture. In Grotowski's version, those scenes are played by prisoners in Auschwitz wearing striped uniforms, and the dialogue is accompanied by tortures. Only the tortures are real, and the sublime language of the verses recited by the actors is sarcastically colored by the very law of contrast.

Putting culture on trial so summarily must provoke serious doubt, for it simplifies the human condition and in that manner departs from truth, as happened in the past with various kinds of Weltschmerz and *mal du siècle*. By living through disintegration in its most tangible varieties, Polish poetry, strange as this may sound, joined once more with Western poetry contaminated by "European nihilism," only to give it a more radical expression. This is true of the poetry of Tadeusz Różewicz, who made his debut after the war. Characteristically, while putting culture on trial, he often makes use of shorthand and symbols borrowed from that culture, as for instance in his poem "Nothing in Prospero's Cloak," a travesty of *The Tempest*. The civilizing power of the wise Prospero who, on his island, introduces Caliban to the world of human speech and good manners proves to be a sham.

Caliban the slave
taught human speech
waits

his mug in dung
his feet in paradise
he sniffs at man
waits

nothing arrives
nothing in Prospero's magic cloak
nothing from streets and lips
from pulpits and towers
nothing from loudspeakers
speaks to nothing
about nothing

Poems of this kind seem to fulfill a surrogate function, that is, they direct a global accusation at human speech, history, and even the very fabric of life in society, instead of pointing out the concrete reasons for the anger and disgust. That probably happens because, as was the case in Poland during war, reality eludes the means of language and is the source of deep traumas, including the natural trauma of a country betrayed by its Allies.

The reality of the war years is a great subject, but a great subject is not enough and it even makes inadequacies in workmanship all the more visible. There is another element which shows art in an ambiguous light. Noble intentions should be rewarded, and a literary work so conceived should acquire a durable existence, but most often the reverse is true: some detachment, some coldness, is necessary to elaborate a form. People thrown into the middle of events that tear cries of pain from their mouths have difficulty in finding the distance necessary to transform this material artistically. Probably in no language other than Polish are there so many terrifying poems, documents of the Holocaust; with few exceptions, these are poems that survived and whose authors did not. Today a reader hesitates between two contradictory assessments. Next to the atrocious facts, the very idea of literature seems indecent, and one doubts whether certain zones of reality can ever be the subject of poems or novels. The tortures of the damned in Dante's *Inferno* were, after all, invented by the author, and their fictitious character is made apparent by form. They do not appear raw, as do the tortures in documentary poems. On the other hand, because they use rhyme and stanzas, documentary poems belong to literature and one may ask, out of respect for those who perished, whether a more perfect poetry would not be a more appropriate monument than poetry on the level of facts.

After the war the annihilation of the Polish Jews appears in the poems of several writers, some of which found their place in anthologies. But, applying severe criteria, one can say that the subject is beyond the authors' capabilities and rises up before them like a wall. The poems are considered good primarily because they move us with their noble intentions. The difficulty of finding a formula for the experience of elemental cruelty is exemplified by the case of Anna Świrszczyńska. She made her debut before the war with a volume of prose poems, quite lovely and refined, which testified to her interest in the history of art and medieval poetry. And no wonder, for she was the daughter of a painter, grew up in a painter's studio, and at the university studied Polish literature. Neither she nor any of her readers could have guessed what purpose would be served one day by her predilection for illuminated manuscripts and miniatures.

During the war, Świrszczyńska lived in Warsaw. In August and September of 1944 she took part in the Warsaw Uprising. For sixty-three days she witnessed and participated in a battle waged by a city of one million people against tanks, planes, and heavy artillery. The city was destroyed gradually, street by street, and those who survived were deported. Many years later Świrszczyńska tried to reconstruct that tragedy in her poems: the building of barricades, the basement hospitals, the bombed houses caving in burying people in shelters, the lack of ammunition, food, and bandages, and her own adventures as a military nurse. Yet those attempts of hers did not succeed: they were too wordy, too pathetic, and she destroyed her manuscripts. (Also, for a long time the Uprising was a forbidden topic, in view of Russia's role in crushing it.) No less than thirty years after the event did she hit upon a style that satisfied her. Curiously enough, that was the style of miniature, which she had discovered in her youth, but this time not applied to paintings. Her book *Building the Barricade** consists of very short poems, without meter or rhyme, each one a microreport on a single incident or situation. This is a most humble art of mimesis: reality, as it is remembered, is paramount and dictates the means of expression. There is a clear attempt to condense, so that only the essential words remain. There are no comparisons or metaphors. Nevertheless, the book is characterized by a high degree of artistic organization, and, for example, the title poem can be analyzed in terms of the rhetorical figures with Greek names that have been used in poetry for centuries—anaphora, epiphora, epizeuxis:

BUILDING THE BARRICADE

We were afraid as we built the barricade
under fire.
The tavern-keeper, the jeweler's mistress, the barber, all of us
cowards.
The servant girl fell to the ground
as she lugged a paving stone, we were terribly afraid
all of us cowards—
the janitor, the market woman, the pensioner.

* English translation by Magnus J. Krynski and Robert A. Maguire (Krakow: Wydawnictwo Literackie, 1979).

The pharmacist fell to the ground
as he dragged the door of a toilet,
we were even more afraid, the smuggler-woman,
the dress-maker, the streetcar driver,
all of us cowards.

A kid from reform school fell
as he dragged a sandbag,
you see, we were really
afraid.

Though no one forced us
we did build the barricade
under fire.

Świrszczyńska often uses the form of a miniature mono-
logue or dialogue to squeeze in as much information as possible. The small poem "A Woman Said to Her Neighbor" contains a whole way of life, the life in the basements of the
incessantly bombed and shelled city. Those basements were
connected by passages bored through the walls to form an underground city of catacombs. The notions and habits accepted
in normal conditions were reevaluated there. Money meant
less than food, which was usually obtained by expeditions to
the firing line; considerable value was attached to cigarettes,
used as a medium of exchange; human relations also departed
from what we are used to considering the norm and were
stripped of all appearances, reduced to their basest shape. It is
possible that in this poem we are moved by the analogy with
peacetime conditions, for men and women are often drawn together not from mutual attraction but from their fear of loneliness:

A woman said to her neighbor:
"Since my husband was killed I can't sleep,
when there's shooting I dive under the blanket,
I tremble all night long under the blanket.
I'll go crazy if I have to be alone today,

I have some cigarettes my husband left, please
do drop in tonight."

Enterprises like Świrszczyńska's, a diary of events reconstructed many years later, are rare in postwar Polish poetry. Another poet, Miron Białoszewski, succeeded in doing the same thing in prose, in his *A Memoir of the Warsaw Uprising.** Previously, his poems had given no indication that their author had the experiences he related in his memoir. Yet, when the book appeared, it shed light on a peculiar quality of his verse. *A Memoir* is a faithful, antiheroic, and nonpathetic description of disintegration: bombed houses, whole streets, human bodies disintegrate, as do objects of everyday use and human perceptions of the world. A witness of that disintegration could not help but write as Białoszewski the poet did afterwards. For a long time he was not published, and no wonder, for it is difficult to find any poetry more distant from the official optimism. His poetry is mistrustful of culture, no less than that of Różewicz, but above all it is mistrustful of language, for language is the fabric from which the garments of all philosophies and ideologies are cut.

One can say that Białoszewski performs a Cartesian opera tion, in the sense that he effects a reduction and attempts to draw a circle, even a small one, around something in which he can believe. He appears to have divided reality into two layers: a higher layer, embracing all that creates culture, namely churches, schools, universities, philosophical doctrines, systems of government and a second, lower layer, life at its most down-to-earth. People go to a store, they use a dish, a spoon, and a fork, sit down on a chair, open and close the door, in spite of what happens up there, "above." They communicate in a language indifferent to correct grammar and syntax, in an idiom of half words, sentences interrupted in the middle, grunts, silences, and peculiar intonations. Białoszewski wants

* English translation by Madeline Levine (Ann Arbor: Ardis, 1977).

to stay within that lower everyday world and its language. He is like a Roman who, witnessing the fall of Rome, seeks help in what is most durable because it is the most elementary and trivial and, for that reason, is able to grow on the ruins of states and empires. The poetry of the last few decades, not only in Poland but everywhere, has renounced meter and rhyme, and has begun reducing words to their components; in this respect, Białoszewski differs only by the radical nature of his attempts. But there is something else in him, an aural mimesis—in the common speech of Warsaw's streets he hears "rustles, snatches, flows," and he jots them down in a nearly inarticulate mumble. In such diction he writes of insignificant daily incidents in his life and that of his acquaintances, mixing verse and prose, though the borderline between them already is so blurred that differentiation becomes meaningless. Taken together, these poems make a chronicle of the streets of the city in which he was born and which he saw destroyed and rebuilt. What is for me most interesting is the democratic quality in Białoszewski. Like the other poets I just discussed, he paradoxically breaks the pattern of bohemia, so that the chasm between the poet and the "human family" ceases to exist. This does not mean that he appeals to everybody, for, in a sense, Białoszewski is a continuator of the avant-garde and an anti-poet. His example indicates that the reintegration of the poet does not mean conformity with the taste of the majority. But Białoszewski himself is not alienated—he speaks as one of the crowd, gives himself no airs, stands at no distance, and maintains cordial relations with the people who appear in his prose-poetry.

A diction that juggles peculiarities of flexion and a great number of suffixes cannot be rendered in a foreign language and, as a rule, Białoszewski is untranslatable, especially since his penchant for fragmentary, stenographic notation has increased with time. One poem from his earlier phase, however, does give an idea of his search for something stable, even if it is as unpretentious as shopping in a store:

A BALLAD OF GOING DOWN TO THE STORE

First I went down to the store
by means of the stairs,
just imagine it,
by means of the stairs.

Then people known to people unknown
passed me by and I passed them by.
Regret
that you did not see
how people walk,
regret!

I entered a complete store:
lamps of glass were glowing.
I saw somebody—he sat down—
and what did I hear? What did I hear?
rustling of bags and human talk.

And indeed,
indeed
I returned.

The experience of disintegration during the war years probably marked Polish poetry so firmly because the order established after the war was artificial, imposed from above and in conflict with those organic bonds that survived, such as the family and the parish church. One striking feature of Polish poetry in recent decades has been its search for equilibrium amid chaos and the complete fluidity of all values, something of sufficiently general importance to deserve attention here. Białoszewski program could be called minimalist.

Taking refuge in the world of objects provided a somewhat similar solution. Human affairs are uncertain and unspeakably painful, but objects represent a stable reality, do not alter with reflexes of fear, love, or hate, and always "behave" logically. Zbigniew Herbert, a quiet, reserved poet with an inclination to calligraphic conciseness, has chosen to explore the world of objects. His example confirms what I have said about Polish poetry's rejoining Western poetry because of the disintegration that confronts them both, even if that disintegration is different in quality and intensity. Herbert is sometimes reminiscent of Henri Michaux, but his "mythopoems," as they have been called (poems on objects), are closest to those of Francis Ponge. One notable difference between the two is Herbert's personal approach to an object and Ponge's withdrawal to the role of impersonal observer. In Herbert's work a space filled with human struggles and suffering gives objects their background, and thus a chair or a table is precious simply because it is free of human attributes and, for that reason, is deserving of envy. Objects in his poetry seem to follow this reasoning: European culture entered a phase where the neat criteria of good and evil, of truth and falsity, disappeared; at the same time, man became a plaything of powerful collective movements expert in reversing values, so that from one day to the next black would become white, a crime a praiseworthy deed, and an obvious lie an obligatory dogma. Moreover, language was appropriated by the people in power who monopolized the mass media and were able to change the meaning of words to suit themselves. The individual is exposed to a double attack. On the one hand, he must think of himself as the product of determinants which are social, economic, and psychological. On the other hand, his loss of autonomy is confirmed by the totalitarian nature of political power. Such circumstances make every pronouncement on human affairs uncertain. In one of Herbert's poems the narrator hears the voice of conscience but is unable to decipher what the voice is trying to say. In another, "The Elegy of Fortinbras," Hamlet loses out because of his "crystal notions," synonymous with being unprepared for life, while practical Fortinbras pronounces an encomium to opportunism. As opposed to the human domain with its shaky foundations, Herbert tells us, objects have the virtue of simply existing—they can be seen, touched, described.

A similar motivation seems to mark the poems of Francis Ponge, except that his turning to objects signifies a desire to go beyond psychology; in Herbert the object is an element of his encounter with History. History is present in an object as an absence: it reminds us of itself by a minus sign, by the object's indifference to it.

THE PEBBLE

The pebble
is a perfect creature
equal to itself
mindful of its limits

filled exactly
with a pebbly meaning

with a secret which does not remind one of anything
does not frighten anything away does not arouse desire

its ardour and coldness
are just and full of dignity

I feel a heavy remorse
when I hold it in my hand

and its noble body
is permeated by false warmth

Pebbles cannot be tamed
to the end they will look at us
with a calm and very clear eye

Mankind, unfortunately, is not "equal to itself." Herbert has read twentieth-century philosophy and knows the definition of man as "he who is what he is not and who is not what he is." It is precisely this that in Sartre makes man foreign to Nature, which is established in itself, equal to itself, and bears another name, "être-en-soi." It is "mindful of its limits," while man is characterized by a limitless striving to transcend all limits. The poem is therefore polemical: it indicates that poetry is not bound to avoid philosophy. So "The Pebble" cannot be numbered among the works of pure poetry.

A pebble is free of feelings, that cause of suffering. It has no memory of past experience, good or bad, and no fear or desire. Human ardor and human coldness can be viewed in a positive or negative light, but in a pebble they are just and full of dignity. Man, transient and short-lived, feels remorse when confronted with a pebble. He is aware that he himself is a false warmth. The last three lines contains a political allusion, though a reader may not notice it at first. Pebbles cannot be tamed, but people can, if the rulers are sufficiently crafty and apply the stick-and-carrot method successfully. Tamed people are full of anxiety because of their hidden remorse; they do not look us straight in the face. Pebbles will look at us "with a calm and very clear eye" to the end. To the end of what? we may ask. Probably to the end of the world. The poems ends on an eschatological note.

A final example of the unexpected turns and transfers by which poetry meets the challenge of history is provided by my late friend Aleksander Wat. Wat has left a monumental work—a memoir, *My Century,* which is currently being translated into English. This book tells of a life rich enough for ten, and of the peculiar dependence of one destiny upon the various philosophies of our century. In his youth, around 1919, Wat was a futurist. Next, in 1927, he published a volume of perverse parable-like tales, *Lucifer Unemployed,* a blatant example of "European nihilism." In 1929 he became editor-in-chief of the major Communist periodical in Poland between the wars, the *Literary Monthly.* After Poland was partitioned by Hitler and Stalin in 1939, Wat found himself in the Soviet zone where he was imprisoned, accused of being a Trotskyite, a Zionist, and an agent of the Vatican. After many years in various prisons and in exile in Soviet Asia, he returned in 1946 to Poland, soon to be accused of departing from the doctrine of socialist realism. And, it should be added, that spiritually he was shaped in equal measure, as he stressed in his memoirs, by Judaism, Catholicism, and atheism.

Wat therefore typifies the numerous adventures of the European mind in its Polish variety, that is, a mind not located in some abstract space where what is elementary—hunger, fear, despair, desire—does not penetrate. Wat experienced the philosophies of the twentieth century bodily, in their most tangible forms. He spent time, as he says himself, "in fourteen prisons, many hospitals, and innumerable inns," always taking on roles imposed by the people in power: the role of a prisoner, a patient, an exile. After his period of youthful futurism he virtually abandoned poetry for a long time. He fulfilled himself as a poet in his old age. His late poems are sort of haphazard notes by a man who is locked inside "the four walls of his pain," physical pain. Moreover, Wat is inclined to see his suffering as a punishment, for he was guilty of a grave sin. That sin, widespread in this century, was defined by Nadezhda Mandelstram in her memoirs when she said that, though much can be forgiven a poet, he must not become a seducer, not use his gifts to make his reader into a believer in some inhuman ideology. Wat passed a severe judgment on his nihilistic operations in the twenties and on his subsequent work as editor of the Communist periodical that had such great influence in Poland.

Capricious, highly subjective notes—such, at least in appearance, are Wat's late poems. He speaks of himself, and yet some unexpected transmutation turns that chronicle of his own afflictions into a chronicle of this century's agonies. Wat's example seems to verify my assumption that once reality surpasses any means of naming it, it can be attacked only in a roundabout way, as it is reflected in somebody's subjectivity. Herbert's poem "The Pebble" applies a specific *via negativa* when he speaks of man's fate and praises inanimate nature which contradicts that fate. Wat's *Mediterranean Poems*, written when he was approaching seventy, are the memories of a castaway, a sick veteran of beliefs and doctrines, who finds himself in the stony landscape of the Alpine foothills and is engaged in a major reassessment. I think it was the German philosopher Adorno who said that, after the Holocaust, poetry is impossible. In Wat's private poetic jottings there is no mention of the Holocaust or of what he, along with more than a million others, lived through during their deportation to Russia. His cry, the cry of Job, tells only of the conclusions drawn by a survivor. As in Herbert, inanimate nature becomes an object of envy.

> Disgusted with everything alive I withdrew into the stone
> world: here I thought, liberated, I would observe from above,
> but
>   without pride, those things
> entangled in chaos. With the eyes of a stone, myself
>   a stone among stones, and like them sensitive,
> pulsating to the turning of the sun. Retreating into
>   the depth of myself, stone,
> motionless, silent; growing cold; present through a waning
>   of presence—in the cold
> attractions of the moon. Like sand diminishing in
>   an hourglass, evenly,
> Ceaselessly, uniformly, grain by grain. Thus I shall be sub-
>   mitted
> only to the rhythms of day and night. But—
> no dance in them, no whirling, no frenzy: only
>   monastic rule and silence.
> They do not become, they are. Nothing else. Nothing
>   else, I thought, loathing
> all which becomes.

What can poetry be in the twentieth century? It seems to me that there is a search for the line beyond which only a zone of silence exists, and that on the borderline we encounter Polish poetry. In it a peculiar fusion of the individual and the historical took place, which means that events burdening a whole community are perceived by a poet as touching him in a most personal manner. Then poetry is no longer alienated. As the etymology of the term suggests, poetry is no longer a foreigner in society. If we must choose the poetry of such an unfortunate country as Poland to learn that the great schism in poetry is curable, then that knowledge brings no comfort. Nevertheless, the example of that poetry gives us perspective on some rituals of the poets when they are separated from "the great human family." Clearly, any neat division of poetry into the "alienated" and "nonalienated" will encounter serious difficulties. I pretend to no precision here.

Mallarmé's sonnet "Le Tombeau d'Edgar Poe," which I have already quoted, is a symbolist manifesto and as such provides some valuable hints. Edgar Allan Poe is called an angel who wanted "donner un sens plus pur aux mots de la tribu," to give a purer meaning to the words of the tribe. Curiously enough, it was precisely Poe's use of English and his form of versification that contributed to his marginal place in the history of American poetry. But a myth needs a conflict between an angel and the hydra of the crowd, and here both Poe's life and the distance between France and America were of help. From romanticism, of course, comes the idealization of the lonely, misunderstood individual charged with a mission in society, and thus French symbolism emerges as a specific mutation of the romantic heritage. Whereas in romanticism a poet had to prophesy, to lead, to move hearts, here we have the idea of purity and defensiveness, opposed to vulgarity and dirt. On the one side, an angel and "un sens plus pur"; on the other, "le flot sans honneur de quelque noir melange," a wave without honor of some black mixture. But the ending of Mallarmé's sonnet is probably crucial: Poe's granite tomb is to remain forever a landmark, not to be crossed by "noirs vols du Blasphème," black flights of Blasphemy.

A landmark that will last forever. Here we can see how Mallarmé's sonnet differs from romanticism. The relationship between the poet and the crowd is defined as stable, not imposed by circumstances that would be changed by historical movement. Society appears as given, like trees and rocks, endowed with the firm, settled existence typical of nineteenth-century bourgeois France. It is precisely that aspect of poetry in isolation as depicted in this sonnet which strikes us as incompatible with what we have learned in the twentieth century. Social structures are not stable, they display great flexibility, and the place of the artist has not been determined once and for all. To be fair to Mallarmé, let us recall that he appears to say exactly the same thing as Horace, who called himself "Musarum sacerdos" (a priest of the Muses) and declared: "Odi profanum vulgus et arceo" (I hate the profane crowd and keep it at a distance). But the similarity is illusory, for we are confronted with two different historical contexts.

Polish poets found out that the hydra so ominously present for the symbolists is in reality quite weak, in other words, that the established order, which provides the framework for the quarrel between the poet and the crowd, can cease to exist from one day to the next. In that light, Mallarmé's sonnet is a typical work of the nineteenth century, when civilization seemed to be something guaranteed. And, of course, Polish poets may reproach their Western colleagues who generally repeat the thought patterns proper to the isolated poet. That would be a reproach for lacking a sense of hierarchy when appraising phenomena or, more simply put, for lacking realism. In colloquial speech, the word "unrealistic" indicates an erroneous presentation of facts and implies a confusion of the important and the unimportant, a disturbance of the hierarchy. All reality is hierarchical simply because human needs and the dangers threatening people are arranged on a scale. No easy agreement can be reached as to what should occupy first place. It is not always bread; often it is the word. And death is not always the greatest menace; often slavery is. Nevertheless, anyone who accepts the existence of such a scale behaves differently than someone who denies it. The poetic act changes with the amount of background reality embraced by the poet's consciousness. In our century that background is, in my opinion, related to the fragility of those things we call civilization or culture. What surrounds us, here and now, is not guaranteed. It could just as well not exist—and so man constructs poetry out of the remnants found in ruins.

6
On Hope

S O far I have dealt with poetry as something entangled in transformations of mentality, in everything we are tempted to call the Zeitgeist, though nobody is able to define it. But now I am going to ask a simple question. What if the lament so widely spread in poetry today proves to be a prophetic response to the hopeless situation in which mankind has found itself? In that case, poetry would have proven once again that it is more conscious than the average citizen, or that it simply intensifies what is always present but veiled in people's minds.

In the nineteenth century the belief in the decline and imminent fall of Western civilization found expression first in Russian thought, and in that respect Dostoevsky is no exception. The same belief was soon to appear in Western Europe. The Parisian review *Le Décadent* said in 1886: "It would be nonsense to conceal the state of decadence that we have reached. Religion, mores, justice, everything is tending toward decline." What was called decadence soon became a movement and a fashion among bohemians, just as existentialism would a few decades later. Also, around 1900 the serene science fiction of Jules Verne was replaced by ominous predictions of general catastrophe or of the rule by machines which elude human control. The Slavic word *robota* entered common usage in various languages as "robot," an invention of the Czech writer, Karel Čapek.

Technology as a subject for science fiction also imperceptibly acquired a political shade, producing images of a future society which were not hopeful. Perhaps a farewell to nineteenth-century optimism had already been made in H. G. Wells's *The Time Machine* (1895), while our century created novels about the totalitarian systems of tomorrow, such as Yevgeny Zamyatin's *We* (1926), Aldous Huxley's *Brave New World* (1932), and George Orwell's *1984* (1948). On an equal footing I would put two novels by Stanisław Ignacy Witkiewicz, which are little known in the West: *Farewell to Autumn* (1927) and *Insatiability* (1930; published in English in 1977). This literature of anticipation corresponds to a universal and nearly obsessive preoccupation with the future, which is understandable, for great changes occur in an individual's immediate environment in the course of a single lifetime. We sense, again, "l'accélération de l'histoire."

It is interesting to reflect on the extent to which certain writers' predictions have been fulfilled. In one sense, Dostoevsky was in appearance only writing about his contemporaries. He said once, "Everything depends upon the twentieth century," and he tried to guess what man would be like then, just as did his adversary Chernyshevsky, whom Lenin was to choose for a master. Dostoevsky, we now see, fully deserves the title of prophet, if only as the author of *The Possessed*. Nevertheless, when reading him we seem to discover the limitations to any prophesying. Such prophecies probably always resemble a column of type that has been skewed, so that the particular lines are changed in order and the sequence of sentences is broken; or to use another comparison, they are like a series of mirrors where it is difficult to tell reality from illusion. That is, all the data are there, correctly foreseen, only their relations and proportions are disturbed. Thus the future is always seen as through a glass, darkly.

Should we also grant the title of prophet, say, to a "decadent" from the last years of the nineteenth century, who read Dostoevsky and Nietzsche, admired Schopenhauer, and sought a remedy to boredom and futility by dreaming of Nirvana? If he chose to commit suicide, a not infrequent occurrence, the events soon to transpire would provide some justification for that act. We still have not fully grasped what the year 1914 meant for Europe and how violently the scales of its destiny were tipped then. The pessimistic poetry written by decadents may just be the future encoded and seen darkly. What actually does come to pass is always a little bit different from our conscious or unconscious expectations, but that "bit" denotes a radical divergence. Too many things have happened since that time not to make the mind-set from 1900 completely foreign to us, even though we recognize that the questions tormenting the decadents were well founded.

Later on, when World War I seemed no more than a cruel episode in the history of Europe, an attempt was made to cultivate a certain myth, which proved to be short-lived and is forgotten today. That was the myth of the Unknown Soldier. Wreaths were laid on his tomb, and many poems were written on the subject. For a while, the myth proved helpful to the rather strong pacifist movements in various countries; allied with the political left, they were unwittingly preparing the ground for the victories of dictators. In the 1920s the same poet would often be the author of poems on the Unknown Soldier and on mustard gas. For it should be remembered that the next war was envisioned as a poison-gas war, and the Yperite, or mustard gas, employed at the end of World War I at Ypres became a symbol like the atomic bomb later on. Here again, the prophecies proved not quite correct. When the next world war broke out, its horrors were of a sort unforeseen by anyone, and neither side made use of gas on the battlefield.

One could make a catalogue of the ominous forecasts appearing today in both science fiction and poetry. In view of an atmosphere conducive to borrowing themes and the uncertain nature of prophecy, we should treat those anxieties with a dose of suspicion. This does not mean that a sober appraisal of the human situation at the end of the twentieth century will be particularly reassuring. And since a poet, as I have said, should be faithful to reality, evaluating it with a sense of hierarchy, I shall not be digressing if I turn my attention for a moment to matters that preoccupy politicians and economists.

We are on the way toward the unification of our planet. For the time being, that unification proceeds in science and technology, which are the same everywhere. This is the result of the victory of a single civilization, the one that arose on the small Western European peninsula. Thanks to the quarrels of its theologians, that civilization developed the mechanism of abstract thought, which was subsequently applied to scientific discoveries. It has overcome and nearly destroyed the more static civilizations, closed in on themselves. A variety of technical inventions, from weapons to the automobile, transistor, and television, were its means of conquest and, by the same token, its philosophical representatives. At the same time, the European peninsula exported its internal crisis, primarily the crisis of its political form, to the whole planet. The scientific-technical revolution took place within the framework of monarchies ruled by kings whose authority had divine sanction, and this presupposed vertical structure: the divine above, the human below. A radical change occurred when the source of authority was shifted to the people, to a "general will" expressed by voting. The model taken by Rousseau from the assemblies of the entire population of a small Swiss canton proved to be more and more abstract when applied in countries with many millions of inhabitants, and as soon as the methods of influencing public opinion began to gain in complexity. If the nineteenth century seemed everywhere to move toward democracy, the twentieth century brought it a series of defeats. Democracy has shown little ability to expand beyond the area of its origin, the Western European peninsula and North America. What is more, the inhabitants of the countries with democratic systems have, in their majority, been affected by a lack of faith in the validity of democracy and in the possibility of defending it against the encroachments of an aggressive totalitarian system.

That system, too, derives the language it uses to sing its own praises from the notion of general will, modifying the notion accordingly. The rulers appear as an incarnation of a general will that, if left to itself, would not know its own true desires. One of the features of totalitarianism, which often cites Karl Marx, is to treat the population as children who shouldn't be allowed to play with matches, that is, to express their opinion in free elections. Yet fictitious elections are preserved, and this reminds us of the Western European origin of democracy's rival. Of course, the basic conflict is camouflaged by making the redistribution of wealth the primary social task. The real quarrel, however, is about the source of authority.

Our planet is small, and its unification into one global state is not unplausible. It could be accomplished, for instance, by conquest. Atomic war is a possibility, yet perhaps no more so than the use of a poison gas was in World War II, and today's pacifist movements are not free of hysteria. Infantry has been a decisive factor in all wars of this century, and this can incline us to suppose it will be decisive in the future as well.

Today the entire earth resembles the Greek peninsula at the time of the Peloponnesian war, at least in the sense that democracy has for its enemy countries that begin the military training of their youth in childhood. Yet both the modern Athens and the modern Sparta are afflicted by grave diseases, and their policies are to a considerable extent marked by their sickliness. A decline of civic virtues is occurring in the West, so that young generations cease to view the state as *their own* (worthy of being served and defended even at the sacrifice of one's life). In this respect, the year 1940 in France set the pattern of peace at any price, even by surrendering to the enemy. Still, that disease and others of a similar kind seem to be related functionally to the West's extraordinary creative capability, as if disintegration were a necessary condition to its progress. A decadent from 1900 would be struck today by the unprecedented development of science, technology, medicine, and the arts, precisely in the era which, according to his predictions, was to see nothing but ruin. And the apparent health of the totalitarian system, with its official cult of the state and the military virtues, conceals the disease of stagnation in every field of human endeavor except arms production. Now, as the century draws to its close, there is no doubt left as to the parasitic character of any state based upon a monopoly of ownership and power. It feeds on what remains from the organic past—not yet completely erradicated—or on technology, science, and art imported from outside. To imagine a worldwide totalitarian state is to imagine a dark age of sterility and inertia.

If European or North American poets cannot bypass the struggle for the planet, whether or not they admit their interest in that question, it is doubtful whether their Latin American colleagues would be able to show so much concern. They seem to live in a different historical time, the time of popular movements in that part of the world, and are unconcerned with things of which an inhabitant of Poland or Czechoslovakia has firsthand knowledge. The nonparallelism of historical times coexisting on earth introduces additional elements into the general human anxiety.

The fate of civilization—the only one, for the others have lost the game—is not comforting, and that is why some poets are now zealous readers of Nostradamus' apocalpytic prophecies. When looking for hope, we must turn to the internal dynamic responsible for having brought us to this precise point.

Things begin to look strange once we reflect on the notions of "health" and of "decay," both of which seem to be highly misleading. Time was out of joint not only for Hamlet but for Shakespeare as well, and it would be difficult to maintain that he exaggerated the case. In fact, by the sixteenth century, the modern era was already at its beginnings, with all the good and evil it was to bring. Since that time, poets have tended to visualize an order located somewhere else, in a different place or time. Such longing, by its nature eschatological, is directed against every "here and now" and becomes one of the forces contributing to incessant change. Is this decay? It undoubtedly is, if it means an inability to relate to existing forms. One may advance the hypothesis that what happens in the West is similar to the processes initiated in an organism by bacteria which are indispensable to its proper functioning. It is possible that the Western branch of civilization disintegrates because it creates, and creates because it disintegrates. The fate of Kierkegaard's philosophy may serve as an example. It grew out of the disintegrations occurring within Christianity, in any case within Protestantism; in turn, his reading of Kierkegaard seems to have influenced Niels Bohr, creator of the quantum theory of the atom.*

It is possible that we are witnessing a kind of race between the lifegiving and the destructive activity of civilization's bacteria, and that an unknown result awaits in the future. No computer will be able to calculate so many pros and cons— thus a poet with his intuition remains one strong, albeit uncertain, source of knowledge. Putting economy and politics aside, I will now return to my own reasons for, if not optimism, then at least opposition to hopelessness.

We can do justice to our time only by comparing it to that of our grandfathers and great-grandfathers. Something happened, whose importance still eludes us, and it seems very or-

* Max Jammer, *The Conceptual Development of Quantum Mechanics* (New York: McGraw-Hill, 1966).

dinary, though its effects will both last and increase. The exceptional quality of the twentieth century is not determined by jets as a means of transportation or a decrease in infant mortality or the birth-control pill. It is determined by humanity's emergence as a new elemental force; until now humanity had been divided into castes distinguished by dress, mentality, and mores. The transformation can be clearly observed only in certain countries, but it is gradually occurring everywhere and causing the disappearance of certain mythical notions, widespread in the past century, about the specific and presumably eternal features of the peasant, worker, and intellectual. Humanity as an elemental force, the result of technology and mass education, means that man is opening up to science and art on unprecedented scale.

My late friend, the Polish writer Witold Gombrowicz, was well aware of this. He had a gift for making insolently simple formulations. "I am generally classified as a pessimist, even a 'catastrophist,' " he said in 1968 in Vence, a year before his death.* "Critics have grown accustomed to thinking that a contemporary literature of a certain standard must necessarily be black. Mine is not black. On the contrary, it is more of a reaction against the sardonic-apocalyptic tone currently in fashion. I am like the baritone in the Choral Symphony: 'Friends, enough of this song. Let more joyous melodies be heard.' " And further:

> alienation? No, let us try to admit that this alienation is not so bad, that we have it in our fingers, as pianists say—in our disciplined, technical fingers which, apart from alienation, give the workers almost as many free and marvelous holidays a year as work days. Emptiness? The absurdity of existence? Nothingness? Don't let's exaggerate. A god or ideals are not necessary to discover supreme values. We only have to go for three days

* *A Kind of Testament,* edited by Dominique de Roux (Philadelphia: Temple University Press, 1973).

without eating anything for a crumb to become our supreme god: it is our needs that are at the basis of our values, of the sense and order of our lives. Atomic bombs? Some centuries ago, we died before we were thirty—plagues, poverty, witches, Hell, Purgatory, tortures . . . Haven't your conquests gone to your head? Have you forgotten what we were yesterday?

To this one may answer that today's hell and today's tortures are not inferior to those of the Middle Ages. Nevertheless, the change Gombrowicz had in mind is real. The difficulty of appraising it correctly comes from a peculiar debasement that follows everything new. Citizens in a modern state, no longer mere dwellers in their village and district, know how to read and write but are unprepared to receive nourishment of a higher intellectual order. They are sustained artificially on a lower level by television, films, and illustrated magazines—media that are for the mind what too small slippers were for women's feet in old China. At the same time, the elite is engaged in what is called "culture," consisting mostly of rituals attended out of snobbery and borne with boredom. Thus elemental humanity's openness to science and art is only potential, and much time will pass before it becomes a fact everywhere.

A poet, however, presupposes the existence of an ideal reader, and the poetic act both anticipates the future and speeds its coming. Earlier I spoke of the lessons of biology and of a reductionist Weltanschauung professed universally today. I expressed the hope that it will be superseded by another vision better adapted to the complexity of the world and of individuals. It seems to me that this will be connected, in one or another way, with a new dimension entered on by elemental humanity—and here I expect some surprise from my audience—the dimension of the past of our human race. This would not seem too probable, since mass culture appears quickly inclined to forget important events and even recent ones, and less and less history is taught in the schools. Let us consider, though, what is happening at the same time.

Never before have the painting and music of the past been so universally accessible through reproductions and records. Never before has the life of past civilizations been so graphically recreated, and the crowds that now visit museums and galleries are without historical precedent. Thus technology, which forces history out of the classroom, compensates, perhaps even generously, for what it is destroying. Daring to make a prediction, I expect, perhaps quite soon, in the twenty-first century, a radical turning away from the Weltanschauung marked principally by biology, and this will result from a newly acquired historical consciousness. Instead of presenting man through those traits that link him to higher forms of the evolutionary chain, other of his aspects will be stressed: the exceptionality, strangeness, and loneliness of that creature mysterious to itself, a being incessantly transcending its own limits. Humanity will increasingly be turning back to itself, increasingly contemplating its entire past, searching for a key to its own enigma, and penetrating, through empathy, the soul of bygone generations and of whole civilizations.

Premonitions of this can be found in the poetry of the twentieth century. In 1900 education was of course the privilege of a small elite and included training in Latin and Greek, remnants of the humanist ideal. Some acquaintance with the poets of antiquity read in the original was also required. That period is closed, and Latin has even disappeared from the Catholic liturgy, with not much chance for revival. But, at the same time, judging by poetry, say Robert Graves's, the past of the Mediterranean—Jewish, Greek, Roman—has begun to have an even more intense existence in our consciousness than it had for our educated predecessors, though in a different way. One could multiply examples from poets. Also, the presence of mythical figures taken from European literature or from literary legend is more vivid than at any previous time, figures such as Hamlet, Lear, Prospero, François Villon, Faust.

From this perspective, it is worthwhile to mention the adventures of one poet, at least a few of whose poems belong to the canon of twentieth-century art and who deserves the name of forerunner, even though his work as a whole is uneven. A Greek from Alexandria, Constantin Cavafy was born in 1863. After many attempts at writing in the spirit of fin-de-siècle, he dared to embrace an idea alien to the highly subjectivist literary fashion of his contemporaries. He identified himself with the entire Hellenic world, from Homeric times up through the dynasty of the Seleucids and Byzantium, incarnating himself in them, so that his journey through time and space was also a journey into his own interior realm, his history as a Hellene. Maybe the impulse came from his familiarity with English poetry, primarily with Robert Browning and his personae taken from Renaissance Italy. Perhaps he had also read the poems of Pierre Louys, *Songs of Bilitis*. Be that as it may, Cavafy's best poems are meditations on the past, which is brought closer so that characters and situations from many centuries back are perceived by the reader as kindred. Cavafy seems to belong in the second half of this century, but this is an illusion resulting from his late arrival in world poetry, through translations. In fact, nearly unknown in his lifetime (though T. S. Eliot published him in his *Criterion*) and only gradually discovered after his death in 1933, he wrote his most famous poems before World War I. "Waiting for the Barbarians" dates from 1898; "Ithaka" in the first version from 1894, in the second from 1910; "King Dimitrios" from 1900; "Dareios" and "In Alexandria, 31 B.C." came a little later, in 1917.

Since I have tried to present my Polish background and have used examples taken from Polish poetry in these lectures, it would perhaps be proper to note that the presence of the Hellenic past in Cavafy is particularly understandable for a Polish poet. The true home of the Polish poet is history, and though Polish history is much shorter than that of Greece, it is no less rich in defeats and lost illusions. In Cavafy's decision to exploit his own Hellenic history, his Polish reader recognizes the idea he had already discovered when reading poets of his own tongue: that we apprehend the human condition with pity and terror not in the abstract but always in relation to a given place and time, in one particular province, one particular country.

I have chosen to quote Cavafy's "Dareios"* probably because the character appearing in it is treated with condescending humor and that character is in addition a poet worrying about fame. He seeks fame both as praise from the lips of a monarch and as recognition from malicious critics. This portrait of a poet from two thousand years ago fits into my slightly ironic approach to my own profession, which may be noticeable in what I have said here about its peculiarities.

DAREIOS

Phernazis the poet is at work
on the crucial part of his epic:
how Dareios, son of Hystaspis,
took over the Persian kingdom.
(It's from him, Dareios, that our glorious king,
Mithridatis, Dionysos and Evpator, descends.)
But this calls for serious thought: Phernazis has to analyze
the feelings Dareios must have had:
arrogance, maybe, and intoxication? No—more likely
a certain insight into the vanities of greatness.
The poet thinks deeply about the question.

But his servant, rushing in,
cuts him short to announce very important news:
the war with the Romans has begun:
most of our army has crossed the borders.

* C. P. Cavafy, *Collected Poems*, translated by Edmund Keeley and Philip Sherrard, edited by George Savidis. Translation © 1975 by Edmund Keeley and Philip Sherrard; reprinted by permission of Princeton University Press.

The poet is dumbfounded. What a disaster!
How can our glorious king,
Mithridatis, Dionysos and Evpator,
bother about Greek poems now?
In the middle of a war—just think, Greek poems!

Phernazis gets all worked up. What a bad break!
Just when he was sure to distinguish himself
with his *Dareios*, sure to make
his envious critics shut up once and for all.
What a setback, terrible setback to his plans.

And if it's only a setback, that wouldn't be too bad.
But can we really consider ourselves safe in Amisos?
The town isn't very well fortified,
and the Romans are the most awful enemies.

Are we, Cappadocians, really a match for them?
Is it conceivable?
Are we to compete with the legions?
Great gods, protectors of Asia, help us.

But through all his nervousness, all the turmoil,
the poetic idea comes and goes insistently:
arrogance and intoxication—that's the most likely, of course:
arrogance and intoxication are what Darcios must have felt.

As we learn from the commentary to Cavafy's poem, the poet
Phernazis is a fictitious character. The city in which he lives,
Amisos, was situated on the shore of Pontus, or the Black Sea.
Mithridatis IV (Evpator) was a king of Pontus, who started a
war with Rome in 71 B.C. and thus it is then that the action of
the poem takes place. Amisos was taken by the Romans three
years later, and King Mithridatis lost the war to Pompeius in
66 B.C.

I have just alluded to identification with people of the past,
to a feeling of fraternity that helps us penetrate the curtain of
time. The poet Phernazis illustrates a secret of the poetic vo-

cation. His worries, as war breaks out and the fate of his city and country is at stake, are comic. And yet, simultaneously with his professional malady—his oversensitivity to favorable opinions of his work—something else takes hold of him: "But through all his nervousness, all the turmoil/the poetic idea comes and goes insistently." A poet cannot break totally away from his little game of pride and humiliation, but at the same time he is liberated, again and again, from his ego by "the poetic idea." All of this acquires a peculiar expressiveness precisely because the city of Amisos, the poet Phernazis, and the king of the realm are for us mere shades asking us to give them life, as the shades of Hades do in Homer.

To make present what is gone by. We are even inclined to believe that a poet receives more than one life just because he is able to walk the streets of a city that existed two thousand years ago. But perhaps it is precisely this that people are seeking in their incessant search for the past in reproductions of old art, in architecture, in fashion, and in crowded museums. A one-dimensional man wants to acquire new dimensions by putting on the masks and dress, the manners of feeling and thinking, of other epochs.

More serious matters seem to be involved here as well. "From where will a renewal come to us, to us who have spoiled and devastated the whole earthly globe?" asks Simone Weil. And she answers, "Only from the past, if we love it." At first sight this is an enigmatic formulation, and it is difficult to guess what she has in mind. Her aphorism acquires meaning in the light of her other pronouncements. Thus she says elsewhere: "Two things cannot be reduced to any rationalism: Time and Beauty. We should start from them." Or: "Distance is the soul of beauty." The past is "woven with time the color of eternity." In her opinion, it is difficult for a man to reach through to reality, for he is hindered by his ego and by imagination in the service of his ego. Only a distance in time allows us to see reality without coloring it with our passions. And reality seen that way is beautiful. This is why the past has such importance: "The sense of reality is pure in it. Here is pure joy. Here is pure beauty. Proust." When quoting Simone Weil I think of what made me personally so receptive to her theory of purification. It probably was not the work of Marcel Proust, so dear to her, but a work I read much earlier, in childhood, and my constant companion ever since—*Pan Tadeusz* by Adam Mickiewicz, a poem in which the most ordinary incidents of everyday life change into a web of fairytale, for they are described as occurring long ago, and suffering is absent because suffering only affects us, the living, not characters invoked by all-forgiving memory.

Humanity will also explore itself in the sense that it will search for reality purified, for the "color of eternity," in other words, simply for beauty. Probably this is what Dostoevsky, skeptical as he was about the fate of civilization, meant when he affirmed that the world will be saved by beauty. This means that our growing despair because of the discrepancy between reality and the desire of our hearts would be healed, and the world which exists objectively—perhaps as it appears in the eyes of God, not as it is perceived by us, desiring and suffering—will be accepted with all its good and evil

I have offered various answers to the question why twentieth-century poetry has such a gloomy, apocalyptic tone. It is quite likely that the causes cannot be reduced to one. The separation of the poet from the great human family; the progressing subjectivization that becomes manifest when we are imprisoned in the melancholy of our individual transience; the automatisms of literary structures, or simply of fashion— all this undoubtedly has weight. Yet if I declare myself for realism as the poet's conscious or unconscious longing, I should pay what is due to a sober assessment of our predicament. The unification of the planet is not proceeding without high cost. Through the mass media poets of all languages receive information on what is occurring across the surface of the whole earth, on the tortures inflicted by man on man, on starvation, misery, humiliation. At a time when their knowledge of reality was limited to one village or district, poets had no such burden to bear. Is it surprising that they are always morally indignant, that they feel responsible, that no promise of the further triumphs of science and technology can veil these images of chaos and human folly? And when they try to visualize the near future, they find nothing there except the probability of economic crisis and war.

This is not the place to say what will happen tomorrow, as the fortune tellers and futurologists do. The hope of the poet, a hope that I defend, that I advance, is not enclosed by any date. If disintegration is a function of development, and development a function of disintegration, the race between them may very well end in the victory of disintegration. For a long time, but not forever—and here is where hope enters. It is neither chimerical or foolish. On the contrary, every day one can see signs indicating that now, at the present moment, something new, and on a scale never witnessed before, is being born: humanity as an elemental force conscious of transcending Nature, for it lives by memory of itself, that is, in History.

Index

Adorno, Theodor, 94
Age of Raptures, 13, 14, 18, 36, 51
Age of Reason, 13, 14, 36
Age of Progress, 18, 51
Akhmatova, Anna, 17
American Civil War, 81
Appollinaire-Kostrowicki, Guillaume, 23
art as art, 46, 49
Artaud, Antonin, 29
Auerbach, Erich, 62–63

Bacon, Francis, 47
Baudelaire, Charles, 18, 26
Beethoven, Ludwig van, 14
Bellay, Joachim du, 10, 62
Bergman, Ingmar, 11
Białoszewski, Miron, 87–89; "A Ballad of Going Down to the Store," 89
Bible, 33, 37, 43, 82. See also Gospels
Blake, William, 13, 24, 25, 28, 33, 47, 57
Bloch, Ernst, 36
bohemia, 18–19, 27, 49, 55, 65, 73, 88, 101
Bohr, Niels, 107
Borwicz, Michał, 67–68, 80
Brecht, Bertolt, 16, 35
Bremond, Henri, 28–29
Browning, Robert, 111
Byron, George Gordon, 32

Čapek, Karel, 102
Carpaccio, Vittore, 74
Cavafy, Constantin, 111–114; "Dareios," 112–113
Chaucer, Geoffrey, 62
Chernyshevsky, N. G., 102
Church, 25, 61–62, 63, 107; influence of in Poland, 4–6, 9–10, 89
classicism: classical education, 5, 110; poetics of, 6, 61–64; as paradise lost, 65–66; struggle with realism, 66–75
Conrad, Joseph, 51

Copernicus, Nicolaus, 42, 43
Courbet, Gustave, 69
cubism, 6

dadaism, 55
Dante Alighieri, 26, 29, 30, 34, 84
Darwin, Charles, 42
Decadent, Le (Paris), 101
Descartes, René, 73
Dostoevsky, Feodor, 6, 17, 36–37, 71, 115; as voice of the underground, 18, 47, 81, 101, 102–103

Einstein, Albert, 24, 32
Eliot, T. S., 14–15, 24, 34, 111
Enlightenment, 13, 14, 49

fauvism, 6
Fedotov, Georgy, 5
Fiore, Joachim di, 12
Flaubert, Gustave, 11, 27
French Revolution, 12, 81
futurism, 69, 92–93

Gauss, Christian, 23
Ginsberg, Allen, 15
Giraudoux, Jean, 64
Goethe, Johann Wolfgang von, 24, 26; Faust, 30, 110
Gombrowicz, Witold, 108–109
Gospels, 45, 63
Graves, Robert, 110
Grosz, George, 16
Grotowski, Jerzy, 82

Halévy, Daniel, 37
Heine, Heinrich, 24
Herbert, Zbigniew, 89–94; "The Pebble," 91
Hitler, Adolf, 36, 81, 92
Hölderlin, Friedrich, 24
Holocaust, 83, 94
Homer, 26, 29, 34, 65, 82, 114; The Iliad, 63, 65

Horace, 5, 6, 62, 63, 65, 96
Hulme, T. E., 34
Huxley, Aldous, 102

Kafka, Franz, 7
Kierkegaard, Sören, 107
Kochanowski, Jan, 6, 61–64, 66, 68, 75; The Dismissal of the Grecian Envoys, 63–64

Lamartine, Alphonse, 26
Lenin, V. I., 102
Lisbon earthquake (1755), 49–51
Lithuania, 9–10, 13, 23; Wilno, 10, 12, 36
Locke, John, 47
Louys, Pierre, 111

Mallarmé, Stéphane, 18, 26, 27, 46, 95–96
Mandelstam, Osip, 17
Mandelstam, Nadezhda, 93
Mann, Thomas, 51
Marx, Karl, 36, 105
Marxism, 10, 15, 28, 35
Mayakovsky, Vladimir, 16, 17, 33
Michaux, Henri, 90
Mickiewicz, Adam, 13–14, 115
Milosz, Czeslaw: "Bypassing rue Descartes," 8; "No More," 72
Milosz, Oscar, 7, 23–35, 37; A Few Words on Poetry, 25–35
Moréas, Jean, 32
Mozart, Wolfgang Amadeus, 11–13

Napoleon Bonaparte, 6, 12, 81
Nazism, 16, 31, 36, 52
Neruda, Pablo, 35
Newton, Isaac, 24, 42, 47
nihilism, 48, 81, 82, 92, 93
Nietzsche, Friedrich, 18, 47–48, 57, 82, 103
Nostradamus, 106

Ortega y Gasset, José, 28
Orwell, George, 102
Ovid, 5

pagan beliefs, 4, 9–10, 42, 63
Paris, cultural influence of, 6–10, 13, 18

Peloponnesian war, 81, 105
Plato, 34, 74
Pléiade, La, 62, 68
Poe, Edgar Allan, 26, 70, 95
Poetry of Fighting Poland, 80
Poland, 3–9, 65; poetry of, 6–7, 10–14, 17, 44, 61–62, 111; German occupation of, 31, 52, 67–68, 79–89; workers' strike of 1980, 31, 61; poetry from 1939 to 1945, 79–97
Ponge, Francis, 90–91
positivism, 18
Poświatowska, Halina, 44
Pound, Ezra, 15, 24, 34
Proust, Marcel, 115
Pushkin, Alexander, 13

Quevedo, Francesco de, 10

Racine, Jean Baptiste, 29
Renaissance, 25, 45–46, 49, 111; poetry of, 4, 70, 75; Kochanowski as Renaissance poet, 61, 66
Rexroth, Kenneth, 23
Rimbaud, Arthur, 11, 18, 42–43
romanticism, 12, 24–26, 49, 95
Ronsard, Pierre de, 61, 62
Rousseau, Jean-Jacques, 104
Różewicz, Tadeusz, 82, 87; "Nothing in Prospero's Cloak," 82–83
Russian Revolution, 15, 16, 33

Sartre, Jean-Paul, 91
Schiller, J. C. F. von, 14
Schopenhauer, Arthur, 102
science, 18, 29; as leading to a new renaissance, 24, 32–33; influence on poetry, 41–57; as unifying force, 104–110, 115–116
Seneca, 62
Sęp-Szarzyński, Mikołaj, 10
Shakespeare, William, 26, 29, 34, 107, 110; The Tempest, 82
Shelley, Percy Bysshe, 32
Shestov, Lev, 42
Spanish Civil War, 16
Spenser, Edmund, 62; The Faerie Queene, 6
Stalin, Joseph, 81, 92

Steiner, George, 45
surrealism, 6, 55
Swedenborg, Emanuel, 33
Świrszczyńska, Anna, 84–87; "Building the Barricade," 85; "A Woman Said to Her Neighbor," 86–87
symbolism, 6, 18–19, 27, 70, 95–96; Oscar Milosz as symbolist, 23, 26
Szymborska, Wisława, 44–46, 48, 56; "Autonomy," 44–45

technology, 34, 68; development of, 18, 50, 57, 104–110, 115–116; as subject for science fiction, 101–102
Thucydides, 81
Tolstoy, Leo, *War and Peace*, 6
totalitarian systems, 16, 51, 55, 90, 102, 105, 106

Valéry, Paul, 9, 56
Vergil, 5, 63
Verne, Jules, 101

Viatte, Auguste, 11
Vitalis, Ianus (of Palermo), 10

Warsaw Uprising (1944), 84–88
Wat, Aleksander, 92–94; *Mediterranean Poems*, 93–94
Weil, Simone, 53–56, 114–115
Weintraub, Wiktor, 62
Wells, H. G., 102
Whitman, Walt, 14, 31, 70
Wilde, Oscar, 32
Witkiewicz, Stanisław Ignacy, 29, 102
World War I, 32, 33, 70, 103, 111
World War II, 17, 33, 64, 103–105; fall of France, 54–56; German occupation of Poland, 31, 52, 67–68; Polish poetry of, 79–97
Wyspiański, Stanisław, 82

Żagary (Wilno), 36–37
Zamyatin, Yevgeny, 102
Zeno of Elea, 66